Edited by Wang Shaoqiang

COLOR Matching

Using Color in Graphic Design

promopress

Combinaisons de couleurs
à impact maximal

Máximo impacto
combinando colores

Máximo impacto
combinando cores

COLOR MATCHING
Using Color in Graphic Design
Combinaisons de couleurs à impact maximal
Máximo impacto combinando colores
Máximo impacto combinando cores

English preface revised by: Tom Corkett
Translators of the preface: Marie-Pierre Teuler French translation /
Jesús de Cos Pinto Spanish translation /
Élcio Carillo Portuguese (Brazilian) translation
Cover design: spread: David Lorente
with the collaboration of Victoria Arias

PROMOPRESS is a brand of:
Promotora de Prensa Internacional S.A.
C/ Ausiàs March, 124
08013 Barcelona, Spain
Phone: +34 93 245 14 64
Fax: +34 93 265 48 83
info@promopress.es
www.promopress.es
www.promopresseditions.com
Facebook: Promopress Editions
Twitter: Promopress Editions @PromopressEd

Sponsored by Design 360°
– Concept and Design Magazine

Edited and produced by
Sandu Publishing Co., Ltd.
Book design, concepts & art direction by
Sandu Publishing Co., Ltd.
info@sandupublishing.com

ISBN 978-84-15967-25-5

Printed in China

CONTENTS

THE POWER AND MYSTERY OF COLOUR

Marta Cutler and Vanessa Eckstein

Few can deny the immense power of colour. It transcends the boundaries of art, design, photography, architecture and fashion. It possesses physical, sensual, spiritual and intellectual qualities.

Throughout history, philosophers, scientists, mathematicians and artists from Pythagoras and Aristotle to Newton and Albers have sought to explain its mysteries. We've all read their theories. We know what yellow does to our mood.

And yet, for all of their systemization and categorization, why a particular shade, or combination of shades, can touch our soul still remains completely and utterly inexplicable.

Tom Wolfe wrote that "logic gives man what he needs. Magic gives man what he wants." Colour is one of the few elements in the world that gives us both. For everything that is tangible about form in life and in design, it is colour that adds the intangible qualities that enchant us. It is a wondrous bridge between the rational and the intuitive.

We use the word *wondrous* deliberately; colour does not exist outside of our perception. It needs our eyes and our brains to decode what we see. Light waves are colourless until the moment they hit our retinas. But once our photoreceptors are activated, they move into the realm of association and our brains declare, "Green grass."

Yet this process isn't quite as black and white as it seems. Colour is a capricious mistress and highly temperamental. As designers, we're intimately aware that the light in which it's viewed and size, shape, placement and adjacent colours will cause imperceptible shifts in what we perceive.

However, we believe that it is within these very subtleties, transitions and points of contradiction that the true power of colour lies. The more you're in touch with its remarkable language, the more you can appreciate, admire and harness it.

Johannes Itten, a painter, designer and teacher and one of the pivotal members of the Bauhaus, wrote that all artistic effects are based on the creation of contrasts. Ironically, allowing dynamic tensions to flourish between colours is exactly what creates the powerful harmonic balance that seduces us and causes us to feel something.

For us, colour is like music. It's no coincidence that the two share a similar vocabulary. Musicians speak of *tonal colour* or *timbre* to describe the mood and atmosphere of a composition. Words like *opaque*, *bright* and *dark* are used. *Dynamic shading* is the term for the louds and softs that breathe life into all musical passages.

Colour used well adds rhythm, pace and shading to an identity, imbuing it with depth and substance and thus ensuring its longevity.

As in music, colour can create a tonal hierarchy, allowing elements that warrant our full attention to be "mezzo forte," and others to whisper "pianissimo" in the background. Josef Albers understood this well. In his work and teachings he continually experimented with levels of intensity and tone to understand their effects and their duality.

Colour is of course what helps to give a brand its unique voice and tone. When you truly understand a brand's essence the colours of an identity reveal themselves almost intuitively. For us, they become what they're meant to be – no more and no less.

With each project, we find ourselves once again being inducted into these beautiful mysteries. We are continually in awe of the extraordinary pool of infinite possibilities and relationships that influence and transform each other. But perhaps what is most wondrous of all is that at the root of all that power are just three primary colours.

POUVOIR ET MYSTÈRE DE LA COULEUR

Marta Cutler et Vanessa Eckstein

Tout le monde, ou presque, reconnaît l'immense pouvoir de la couleur. Elle transcende les frontières de l'art, du design, de la photographie, de l'architecture et de la mode. Elle possède des qualités physiques, sensuelles, spirituelles et intellectuelles.

À travers l'histoire, philosophes, scientifiques, mathématiciens et artistes, de Pythagore et Aristote à Newton et Albers, ont tenté de percer ses mystères. Nous connaissons leurs théories et nous savons que notre humeur est sensible aux couleurs.

Et pourtant, malgré leurs systèmes et leurs catégories, nous sommes toujours incapables d'expliquer pourquoi une nuance particulière ou une combinaison de teintes donnée est capable de nous toucher jusqu'au plus profond de notre être.

Tom Wolfe a dit que la logique fournit à l'homme ce dont il a besoin alors que la magie lui apporte ce à quoi il aspire. La couleur est l'un des rares éléments existants qui nous procure les deux. Dans la vraie vie et dans le monde de la création, tous les aspects tangibles d'une forme sont moins importants que les qualités intangibles que confère la couleur et qui nous enchantent. La couleur est un pont merveilleux entre la raison et l'intuition.

Nous employons à dessein le mot « merveilleux », parce que la couleur tient du prodige, elle n'existe pas en dehors de notre perception. Elle a besoin de nos yeux et de notre cerveau pour devenir réalité. Les ondes lumineuses sont incolores jusqu'au moment où elles atteignent notre rétine. Mais une fois que nos photorécepteurs sont activés, ils passent en mode association, et notre cerveau signale « herbe verte », par exemple.

Toutefois, le processus n'est pas aussi tranché qu'il paraît. La couleur est une maîtresse capricieuse qui n'en fait qu'à sa tête. Nous savons très bien, nous autres designers, que la lumière ambiante, la taille, la forme, la position et les couleurs adjacentes créent d'infimes variations qui influent sur ce que nous percevons.

Nous croyons cependant que la véritable force de la couleur réside justement dans ces transitions subtiles et ces points de contradiction imperceptibles. À mesure que l'on découvre ce langage extraordinaire, on l'apprécie et on l'admire de plus en plus, et on apprend à le contrôler.

Johannes Itten, peintre, designer, professeur et membre éminent du Bauhaus, a écrit que tous les effets artistiques reposent sur la création de contrastes. Paradoxalement, c'est lorsqu'on laisse les tensions dynamiques se développer entre les couleurs que se produit un équilibre harmonieux dont la puissance nous séduit et qui déclenche en nous des émotions.

Pour nous, la couleur est comme la musique, et ce n'est pas un hasard si elles partagent le même vocabulaire. Les musiciens parlent de « couleur tonale » ou de « timbre » pour décrire l'ambiance et l'atmosphère d'une composition. Ils utilisent des mots tels que *opaque*, *brillant* et *obscur*. On parle de *nuances dynamiques* pour évoquer les temps forts ou doux d'un passage musical.

Lorsqu'elle est utilisée à bon escient, la couleur communique du rythme, de l'allure et de la nuance à une identité. Elle lui confère de la profondeur et de la substance qui seront garantes de sa longévité.

Comme en musique, la couleur est capable de créer une hiérarchie tonale en laissant certains éléments capter toute notre attention avec un « mezzo forte », alors que d'autres plus subtils évolueront « pianissimo » à l'arrière-plan. Josef Albers avait bien compris cela. Ses travaux et ses leçons ont exploré les niveaux d'intensité et de tonalité afin de comprendre leurs effets et leur dualité.

La couleur est bien entendu l'élément qui permet à une marque de se distinguer par son ton et son registre unique. Lorsque l'on comprend vraiment l'essence d'une marque, les couleurs et l'identité se révèlent sans effort de manière intuitive. Pour nous, elles sont exactement ce qu'il fallait, ni plus ni moins.

Chaque projet nous replonge dans cet incroyable univers plein de mystères. Nous sommes toujours émerveillées face aux possibilités et combinaisons infinies qui s'influencent et se transforment l'une l'autre. Mais ce qui est le plus extraordinaire finalement, c'est qu'à la base, il n'y a que trois couleurs primaires.

EL PODER Y EL MISTERIO DEL COLOR

Marta Cutler y Vanessa Eckstein

Pocos pueden negar el inmenso poder del color. El color trasciende los límites entre arte, diseño, fotografía, arquitectura y moda, y posee cualidades físicas, sensuales, espirituales e intelectuales.

A lo largo de la historia, filósofos, científicos, matemáticos y artistas, desde Pitágoras y Aristóteles hasta Newton y Albers, han tratado de explicar sus misterios. Todos hemos leído sus teorías; ya sabemos cómo influye el amarillo en nuestro estado de ánimo.

Y, aún así, pese a toda la clasificación y sistematización, sigue siendo completamente inexplicable por qué un matiz o una cierta combinación nos llegan al alma.

Tom Wolfe escribió que "la lógica le da al hombre lo que necesita. La magia le da lo que desea". El color es uno de los pocos elementos en el mundo que nos da ambas cosas. Entre todos los elementos tangibles relacionados con la forma, en la vida y en el diseño, el color es lo que añade esas cualidades intangibles que nos hechizan. Es un puente prodigioso entre lo racional y lo intuitivo.

Hemos usado la palabra *prodigioso* a propósito: el color no existe fuera de nuestra percepción. Requiere que nuestros ojos y nuestro cerebro descodifiquen lo que vemos. Las ondas de luz son incoloras hasta el momento en que alcanzan nuestra retina; sólo cuando se activan los fotorreceptores, las ondas pasan al reino de la asociación y nuestro cerebro dice: "verde hierba".

Pero no es un proceso tan simple como parece. El color es una amante caprichosa y muy temperamental. Como diseñadores, todos sabemos por experiencia propia que la luz, el tamaño, la posición y los colores adyacentes causan cambios imperceptibles en el color que vemos.

No obstante, creemos que el verdadero poder del color reside precisamente en esas extremas sutilezas, transiciones y puntos de contradicción. Cuanto más nos acercamos a su notable lenguaje, mejor podemos apreciarlo, admirarlo y manejarlo.

El pintor Johannes Itten, diseñador, profesor y miembro señero de la Bauhaus, escribió que todos los efectos artísticos se basan en la creación de contrastes. Paradójicamente, el poderoso equilibrio armónico que nos seduce y nos hace sentir cosas se produce cuando dejamos que broten las tensiones dinámicas entre los colores.

Para nosotras el color es como la música. No es casualidad que ambos compartan un vocabulario similar. Los músicos hablan de *color tonal o timbre* para describir el sentimiento o la atmósfera de una composición. Usan palabras como *opaco*, *brillante* y *oscuro*. *Matiz dinámico* es el término empleado para aludir a los contrastes de fuerza y suavidad que insuflan vida a todo pasaje musical.

El color bien empleado aporta ritmo, compás y matiz a una identidad, la imbuye de profundidad y sustancia y de este modo garantiza su longevidad.

Igual que ocurre en la música, el color puede crear una jerarquía tonal de manera que los elementos que captan nuestra plena atención pueden ser *mezzo forte* mientras que otros elementos susurran un *pianissimo* al fondo. Josef Albers lo entendió muy bien y experimentó continuamente, en sus obras y en sus enseñanzas, con los niveles de intensidad y de tono para comprender sus efectos y su dualidad.

El color es, desde luego, lo que ayuda a darle una voz y un tono únicos a una marca. Cuando entendemos de verdad la esencia de una marca, los colores de su identidad se revelan casi de forma intuitiva. Para nosotras, se convierten en lo que tienen que ser, ni más ni menos.

En cada nuevo proyecto nos vemos, una vez más, sumergidas en estos bellos misterios. Necesitamos continuamente ese extraordinario mar de posibilidades infinitas y de relaciones que se influyen y transforman mutuamente. Pero quizá lo más prodigioso de todo sea que en la raíz de todo ese poder no hay nada más que tres colores primarios.

O PODER E O MISTÉRIO DA COR

Marta Cutler e Vanessa Eckstein

Poucos podem negar o imenso poder da cor. A cor transcende os limites entre arte, desenho, fotografia, arquitetura e moda, e possui qualidades físicas, sensitivas, espirituais e intelectuais.

Ao longo da história, filósofos, cientistas, matemáticos e artistas, desde Pitágoras e Aristóteles até Newton e Albers, trataram de explicar os seus mistérios. Todos nós lemos as suas teorias; já sabemos como o amarelo influi em nosso estado de ânimo.

E, mesmo assim, apesar de toda a classificação e sistematização, continua sendo completamente inexplicável por que um matiz ou uma certa combinação tocam a nossa alma.

Tom Wolfe escreveu que "a lógica dá ao homem o que ele necessita. A magia lhe dá o que ele deseja". A cor é um dos poucos elementos no mundo que nos dá ambas as coisas. Dentre todos os elementos tangíveis relacionados com a forma, na vida e no desenho, a cor é o que agrega essas qualidades intangíveis que nos enfeitiçam. É uma ponte prodigiosa entre o racional e o intuitivo.

Usamos a palavra *prodigiosa* de propósito: a cor não existe fora da nossa percepção. Ela requer que os nossos olhos e o nosso cérebro decodifiquem o que vemos. As ondas de luz são incolores até o momento em que alcançam a nossa retina; só quando são ativados os fotorreceptores, as ondas passam ao reino da associação e o nosso cérebro diz: "grama verde".

Mas não é um processo tão simples como parece. A cor é uma amante caprichosa e muito temperamental. Como desenhistas, todos nós sabemos por experiência própria que a luz, o tamanho, a posição e as cores adjacentes provocam mudanças imperceptíveis na cor que vemos.

Não obstante, acreditamos que o verdadeiro poder da cor está precisamente nessas extremas sutilezas, transições e pontos de contradição. Quanto mais nos aproximamos de sua notável linguagem, melhor podemos apreciá-la, admirá-la e manejá-la.

O pintor Johannes Itten, desenhista, professor e membro sênior da Bauhaus, escreveu que todos os efeitos artísticos baseiam-se na criação de contrastes. Paradoxalmente, o poderoso equilíbrio harmônico que nos seduz e nos faz sentir coisas é produzido quando deixamos que brotem as tensões dinâmicas entre as cores.

Para nós, a cor é como a música. Não é casualidade que ambas compartilhem um vocabulário similar. Os músicos falam da *cor tonal* ou *timbre* para descrever o sentimento ou a atmosfera de uma composição. Utilizam palavras como *opaco*, *brilhante* e *escuro*. *Matiz dinâmico* é o termo usado para aludir a os contrastes de força e suavidade que insuflam vida a toda passagem musical.

A cor bem utilizada acrescenta ritmo, compasso e matiz a uma identidade, impregna-a de profundidade e substância e, deste modo, garante a sua longevidade.

O mesmo acontece na música, a color pode criar uma hierarquia tonal de tal maneira que os elementos que captam toda a nossa atenção podem ser *mezzo forte* enquanto que outros elementos sussurram um *pianissimo* ao fundo. Josef Albers o entendeu muito bem e o experimentou continuamente, em suas obras e em seus ensinamentos, com os níveis de intensidade e de tom para compreender os seus efeitos e a sua dualidade.

A color é, claramente, o que ajuda a dar uma voz e um tom únicos a uma marca. Quando entendemos de verdade a essência de uma marca, as cores de sua identidade se revelam quase de forma intuitiva. Para nós, convertem-se naquilo que devem ser, nem mais nem menos.

Em cada novo projeto nos vemos, uma vez mais, submersas nestes belos mistérios. Necessitamos continuamente desse extraordinário mar de possibilidades infinitas e de relações que se influem e transformam mutuamente. Mas talvez o mais prodigioso de tudo seja que na raiz de todo esse poder não há nada além de três cores primárias.

Vada Media
Brand Identity

For this project, Very Own Studio was asked to re-brand Vada Media, a company that helps businesses and organiztions make the most of media opportunities. The brief was to produce a modern, stylish visual identity that would communicate the Vada Media ethos. The core areas of the business were identified and color coded: PR, training, copywriting, presenting and speaking. Once this brand structure was established, work could begin on the visual elements such as the logo. The simple logo is the perfect foil for the bright colors that represent the brand and services.

Design: Very Own Studio

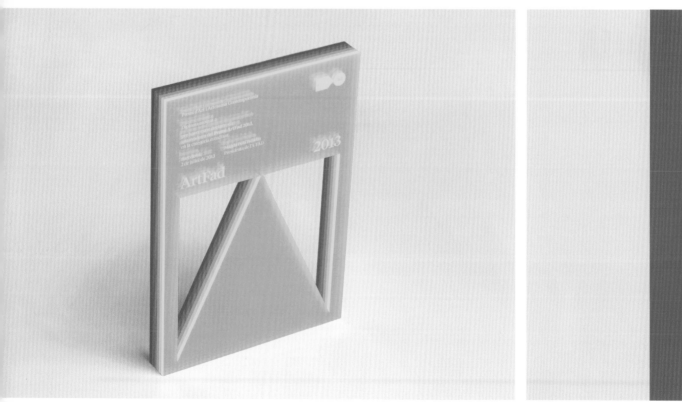

ArtFad 2013 Diploma

ArtFad 2013 Diplomas for the Contemporary Art and Craft Awards. Transparent and fluorescent methacrylate with a laser cut to create the letter "A".

Design: Hey / Photography: Roc Canals

Plua®

Plua® is a real estate company placed in Rio de Janeiro, Brazil. For more than five years Plua has been an industry leader in the South American real estate market. Over this period, Plua's documented real estate excellence in more than ten countries. Design agency Empatia® was asked to design the new identity of this company. The client's main objective was not only to present a company with a strong and modern branding, but also to reflect the vibrant colors and life of Rio de Janeiro. The concept of this branding was based on color. The logo was symbolized by two forms which indicated union and connection. The contrast created by the combination of colors gave the new identity a very fresh, powerful and vibrant look.

Design: Empatia®

Neubau Branding

NEUBAU is a project organized by Microgiants, a Vienna-based design and consulting company covering all aspect of design innovation. NUEBAU, an "awesome temporary design shop," focuses on small productions, innovative design and local Austrian designers. The task was to design the logo and all the branding material for the shop. The leading element of the whole project is the color gradient yellow-fluo pink which is used on all the printed material and on the facade of the shop as well. The pop-up store appeared for the first time in Vienna from October until December 2013.

Design: Cristina Bianchi / Facade Painting: Emanuel Jesse
Interior Design: Franz Piffl, Lukas Bast / Web Design & Development: Vincent Bauer

Ostecx Créative Identity

The new visual identification of Ostecx Créative stands for contrast and simplicity, supplementing minimalistic lettering with embossing and fluorescent gradients. The word "Bonjour" was used to emphasize one of the agency's founders' French roots and invite people to contact them. Intensive colors symbolized energy of their actions and diffusion between the world of design and advertising in the agency's offer. All materials were printed on paper Cyclus Offset.

Design: Ostecx Créative

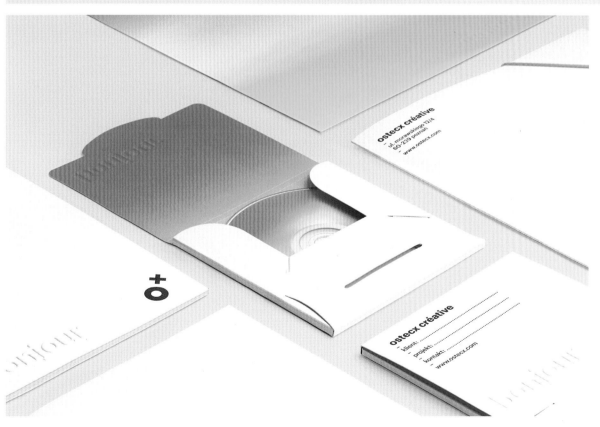

Swish®

White, yellow and blue. Design agency Empatia® gave this new brand a whole graphic universe. Pure and simple. Professional and playful. Swish® is a Sweden seafood company that offers premium fresh fish and seafood from the waters of Sweden, including fresh oysters, herrings, sardines and the authentic flavors of seasonal and local produce.

From the ocean to your plate, Swish® has demanded perfection. In order to achieve this perfection, Empatia® developed a deeper process of branding, revealing unexpected opportunities for this new company, and giving the client opportunities beyond the expected.

Design: Empatia®

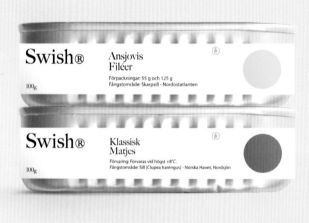

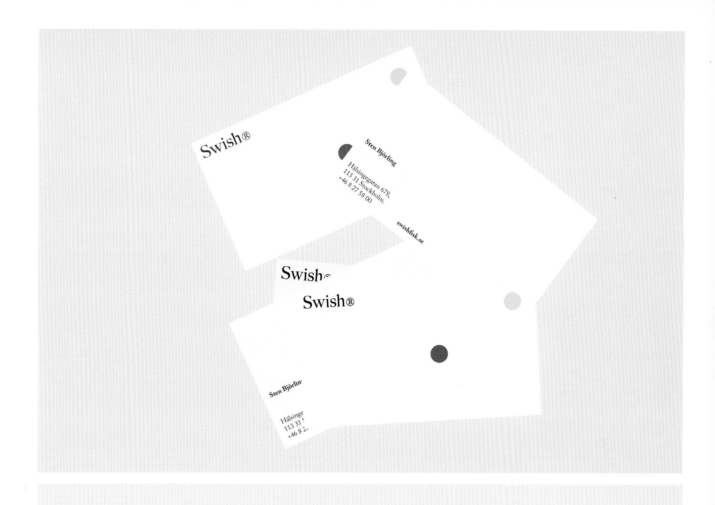

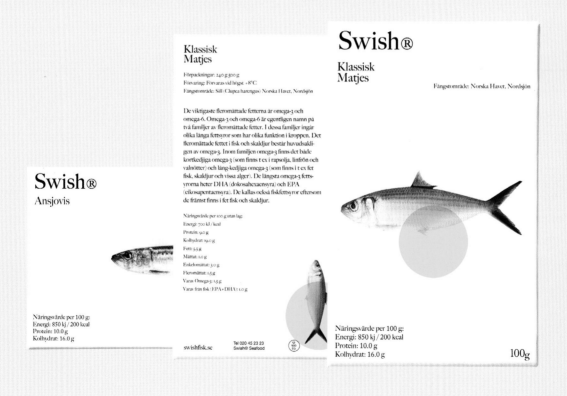

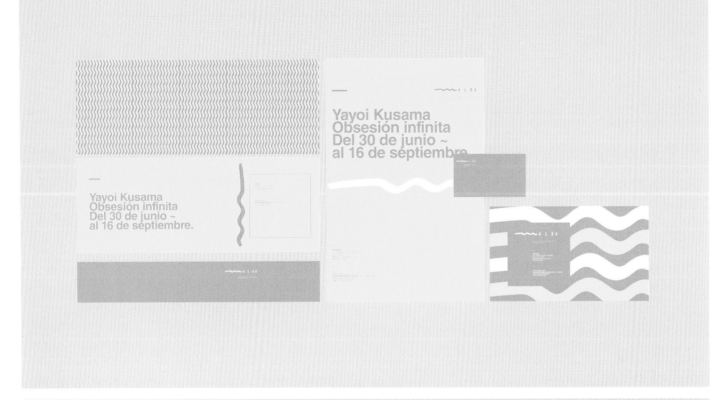

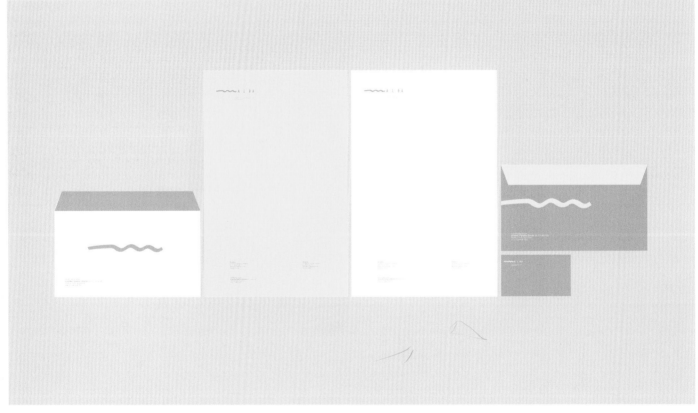

~Alba

Simplicity, elegance, and pureness are the three words that perfectly summed up this project. This design served as a proposed identity for The Latin American Art Museum of Buenos Aires (MALBA), playing with two harmonious colors and a morphologically simple logo. With strong typographic presence and concise order, it reflected a kind of pure, modern and rhythmic character, and most importantly forcefulness.

Design: Maximiliano Passarelli

TenOverSix

TenOverSix is a Los Angeles-based boutique offering a selection of high-concept designer fashion accessories and lifestyle goods. When the boutique evolved to encompass a second location in Dallas, TX, design agency RoAndCo refreshed all the elements of the existing brand collateral – from shopping bags and notecards to garment bags and tissue paper – with a new citrus color palette. For the notecards, they spray painted the edges from corner to corner; when stacked, the sunshiny gradient is visible from the side as well, adding a playful touch.

Design agency: RoAndCo / Creative Direction: Roanne Adams
Design: Verena Michelitsch, Ryan De Remer
Illustration: Verena Michelitsch

Partners for Mental Health

Partners for Mental Health is an organization dedicated to transforming mental health in Canada. The issue is complex, their goal visionary. First, the designers ran the name together to create a feeling of inclusiveness – they are all in this together. Next, they graded the colors to suggest the spectrum of mental health issues. A spirit of change and an element of surprise were crucial to the identity; this transformation cannot be achieved without boldness. Therefore, color is applied vividly and unexpectedly, while language emphasizes the brand's mission. Embedded throughout is a sense of hope, critical to the movement's success.

Design Agency: Blok Design
Creative Direction: Vanessa Eckstein, Marta Cutler
Design: Vanessa Eckstein, Patricia Kleeberg
Copywriter: Marta Cutler

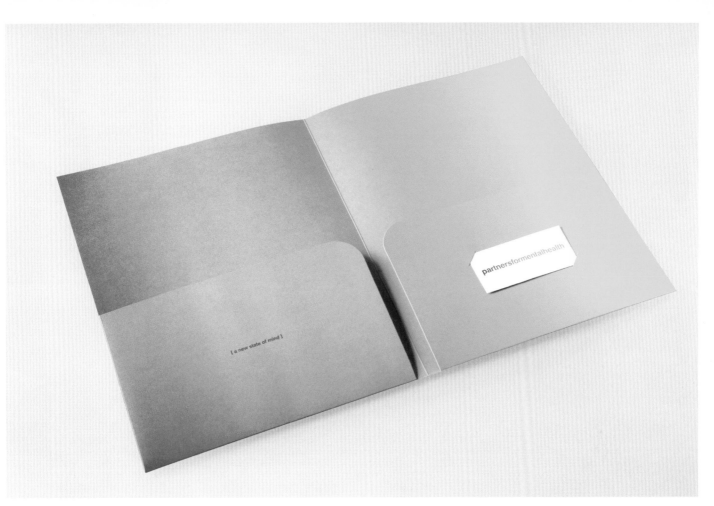

[a new state of mind]

partnersformentalhealth

partnersformentalhealth

tlhealth

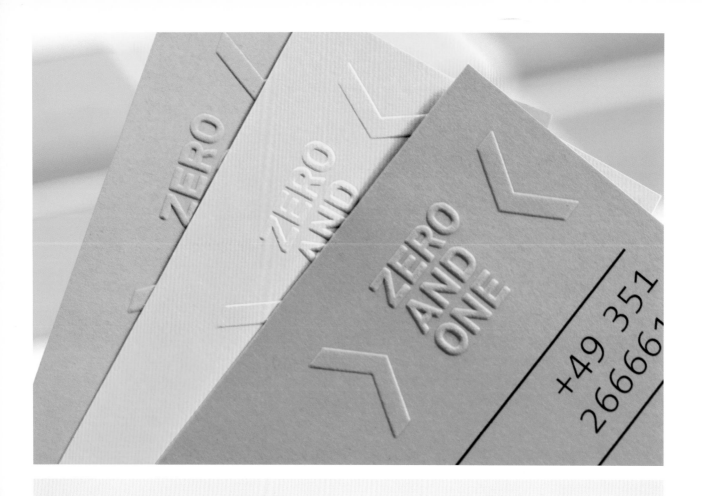

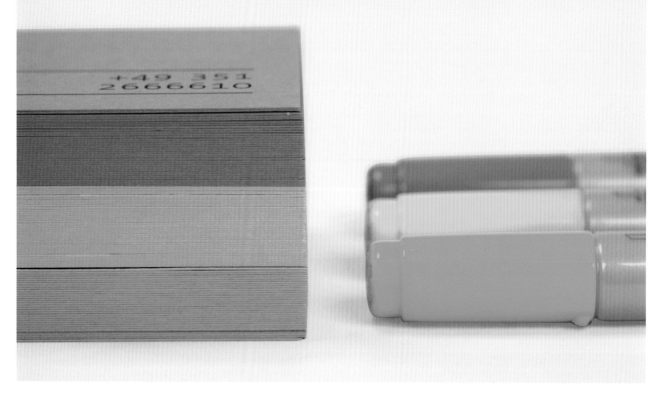

028

Visualworx Identity

ATMO Designstudio created the branding and stationery set for the Dresden-based web developer Visualworx. Smart and eye-catching, this identity used tactile and colorful hues.

Design: ATMO Designstudio

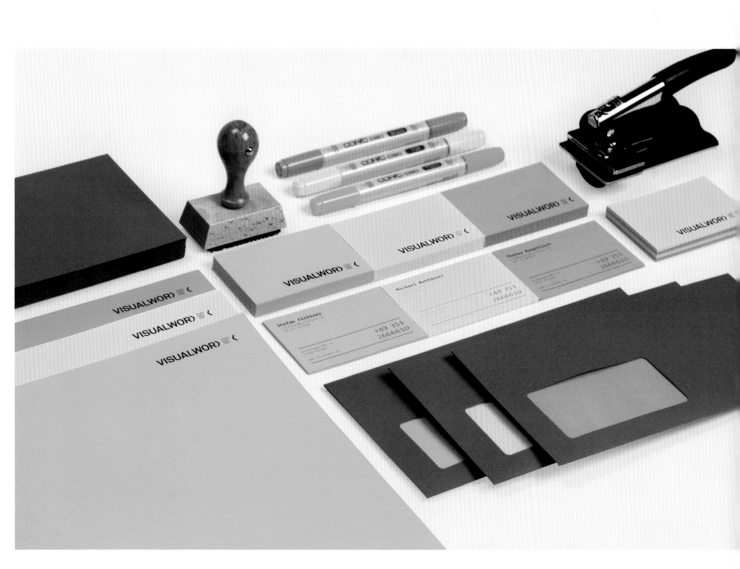

Annual Report for Can Xalant 09/10

The publication included all activities realized by the arts center Can Xalant from 2009 to 2010. Each book was in a different language (Catalan, Spanish and English).
On the cover there was a color gradient to create a connection between these three books, although every one also worked independently. Inside there was a color associated to every language. The images were shifted below the text, appearing only when text columns left an empty space.

Design: Albert Ibanyez

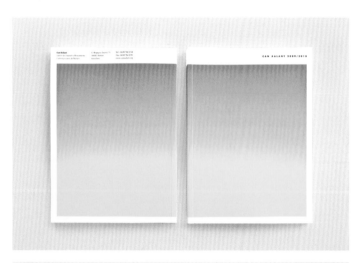

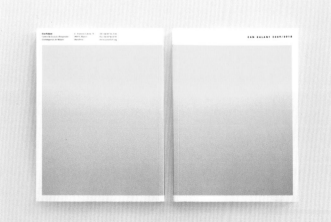

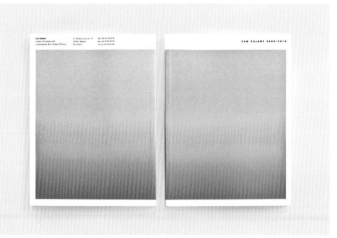

Eating by Design

For the exhibition De Etende Mens, the exhibition graphics were designed by Raw Color. Panels were inspired by commercial signing and supermarket shelves. These panels served as the carriers of information. Eleven different shades, which were carefully chosen, were applied on CNC milled ply wood. The tile of the show was highlighted from behind by fluorescent tubes. Eating by Design explored all avenues of food design from the history of industrial production to the future of man-made proteins. Food Culture will showcase work by designers who concern themselves with the links between design, food, and the origins of what we eat.

Client: Premsela / Design: Raw Color / Curation: Marije Vogelzang, Koos Flinterman
Project Management: Floor van Ast / Exhibition Coordination: Jeroen Wand / Photography: Raw Color

032

Lexington Avenue Agency

Other than professionalism and elegance, Lexington Avenue Agency breathes an urban and sophisticated air. Design studio Masquespacio created a model agency inspired by New York's famous Lexington Avenue. Created from the corporate image, the interior design perfectly reflected the office identity. In this way, the agency strengthened the brand identity and delivered a subliminal message to their visitors.

Design Agency: Masquespacio / Design: Ana Hernández Palacios
Photography: Araski Kuro, David Rodríguez Pastor

Just in Case

Expecting a beautiful chaos, Mexican branding company MenosUnoCeroUno created a survival kit that includes chocolate and hard liqueur to face the apocalypse in style. Packaged in yellow and black, the Just in Case kit also includes more practical items like matches, a knife and water, plus a notebook in case people start to feel philosophical or need to light a fire. Just in Case – the perfect brand for the end of times.

Design Agency: MenosUnoCeroUno / Design: Emmanuel Moreau, Gerardo Ortiz
Photography: Emmanuel Moreau, Gerardo Ortiz

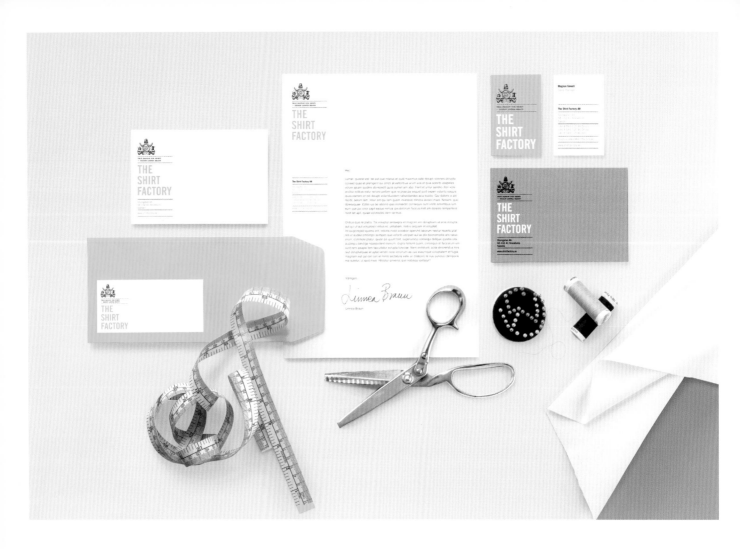

The Shirt Factory

Design agency Bold was asked to create a new visual identity for The Shirt Factory that should revitalize the brand to the Swedish market. The project included a new logotype, color palette, patterns, signage, packaging, etc. A strong yellow color and a crest made up of tailoring equipment are the main carriers of the new identity. The crest suggests quality and attention to detail, and the yellow color suggests a youthful cockiness and makes it stand out among the competition of the market.

Design: Bold Stockholm
Creative Direction: Oskar Lübeck

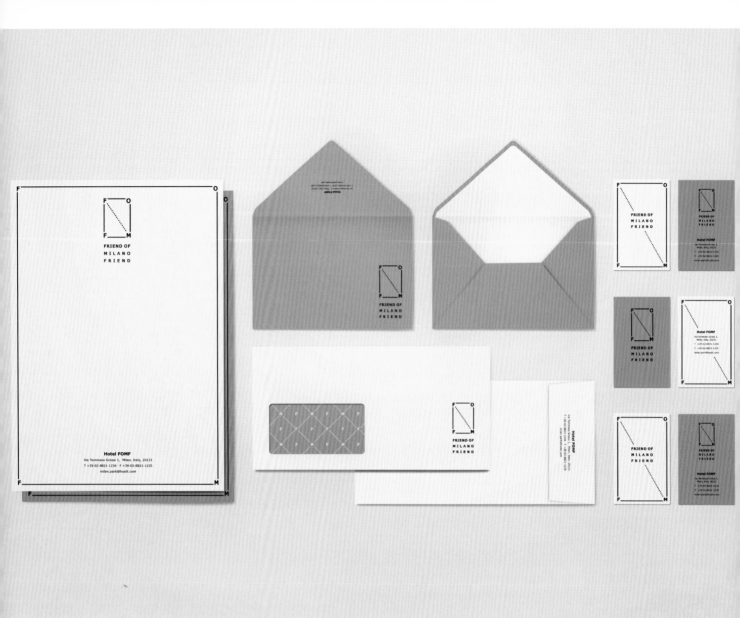

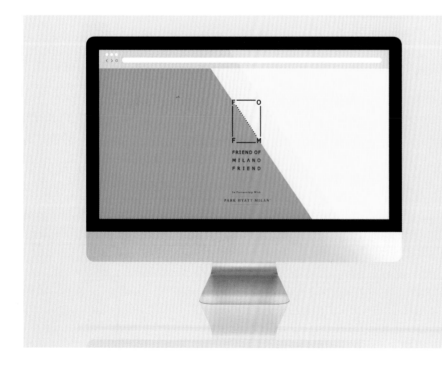

Hotel FOMF

The inspiration for this project came from a term commonly used in cities, "friend-of-a-friend." The idea was to create an experience that would inspire customers to feel as if they were thinking of a friend in Milan when thinking about this new Milan-based hotel. After experiencing the casual but still respectful atmosphere, customers would tell their friends, who in turn would tell their own friends. When the word was out, it would be like friends from every corner of the world were gathering in this hotel in Milan.

Design: Ray Yen

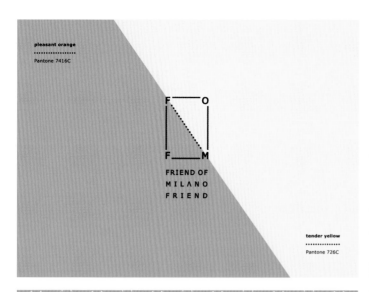

pleasant orange
Pantone 7416C

FRIEND OF
MILANO
FRIEND

tender yellow
Pantone 726C

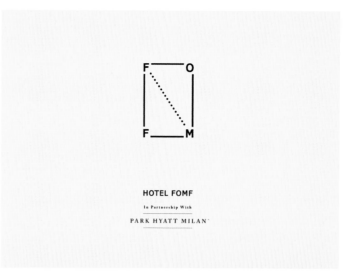

HOTEL FOMF

In Partnership With

PARK HYATT MILAN

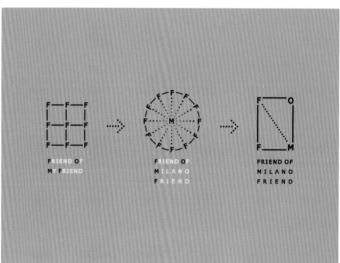

FRIEND OF
MY FRIEND

FRIEND OF
MILANO
FRIEND

FRIEND OF
MILANO
FRIEND

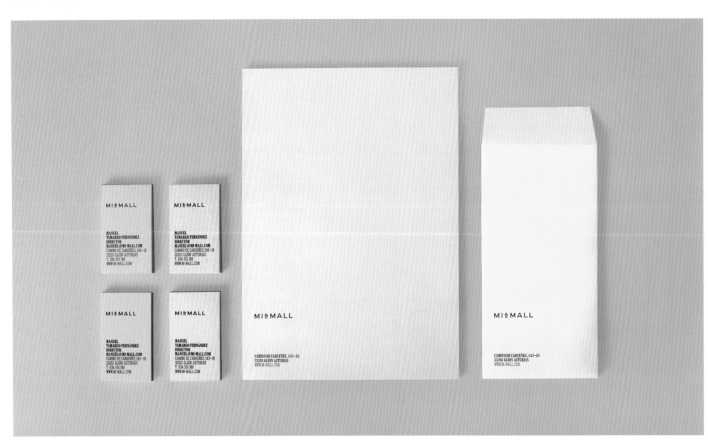

Mi&Mall

Mi&Mall is a new online shopping destination and resource that brings together and supports small to medium designer brands for people interested in fashion, trends and exclusive collections. Their visual identity mixed high fashion cues and craft aesthetics to deliver style and exclusivity with a sense of handmade quality and individuality. It included a simple logo-type, a detailed ampersand, a pale color palate, a tactile print and a crafted material choice.

Design: atipo

Fatties

Design studio Dot Dash worked with the founder of Fatties to develop the name and identity for this new Bakery/Confectionery. Fatties produce their treats from a small bakery at the back of Broadway market, London. The studio created the name and design simultaneously with the idea of juxtaposing the connotations of the name with a clean, sophisticated design. This was done by playfully stretching the letters in the logos, combined with a modern colors scheme and a pattern/texture evoking the floured surfaces seen in bakeries. The overall objective was to produce an identity that was luxurious, playful and modern. To further express the brand they art directed promotional images to complete the visual identity.

Design Agency: Dot Dash / Design: Laura Walpole, Justin Hallstrom
Photography: Jessica Nerstrand

Romero+McPaul

Romero+McPaul is a premium brand specializing in the sale and design of traditional English-style velvet slippers induced with a bright, trendy twist. The inspiration behind this project was drawn from traditional English types and coat of arms mixed with the over-the-top luxuriousness of The Hamptons and its sailing and yacht club maritime lifestyle.

With the intention to speak of the product's duality, a storyline was created based on two characters, Romero and McPaul. Romero is the mischievous heartthrob, representing the product's playfulness, warmth and latino heritage, while McPaul is the serious, traditional man, embodying the product's ancestral and upscale British nature. The rosemary (or "romero" in Spanish) not only serves as a wink to its name but also works as a reference to this herb's curious nature, as it only grows close to the sea.

Design: Anagrama
Photography: Caroga Photographer (branding), Marco+Chuy (shop interiors)

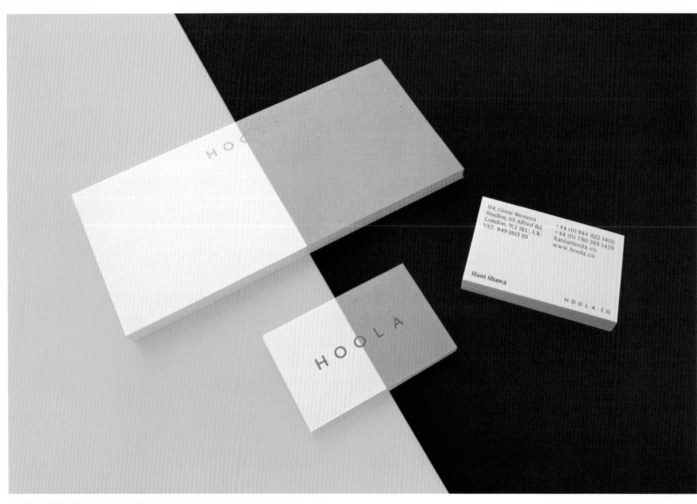

Hoola

Hoola is a women's swimwear brand specializing in D plus cup-sized swimsuit, based in West London. Design agency Two Times Elliott was approached to do an identity refresh as well as a full collateral set and supporting material for the products themselves. The idea behind the identity was that of a horizon. Finished in a Fluorescent Yellow with a Bronze Metallic Foil, the core element of the identity shows the block of color that always dissects the central "O" in Hoola.

Design: Two Times Elliott / Photography: Scott Grummett

Cocolobo

Cocolobo is a high-end shopping boutique that caters exclusively to strong women with a confident and in vogue fashion sense. The name is relative to the shop's main patrons' characteristic duality: "Coco" (coconut in Spanish) and "lobo" (Spanish for wolf). The color palette also invests in this polarity, with black and white portraying the elegant, sober aspect of the brand and the red representing all that is feminine and chic. The layout is modern and simple while the typographic palette emits exclusivity, rounding up the brand as one with dignity and class.

In direct and striking contrast stands the heart icon and pattern, rendering a luscious playfulness and channeling the brand to the world of lipstick loaded kisses and little red dresses.

Design: Anagrama
Photography: Caroga Photographer

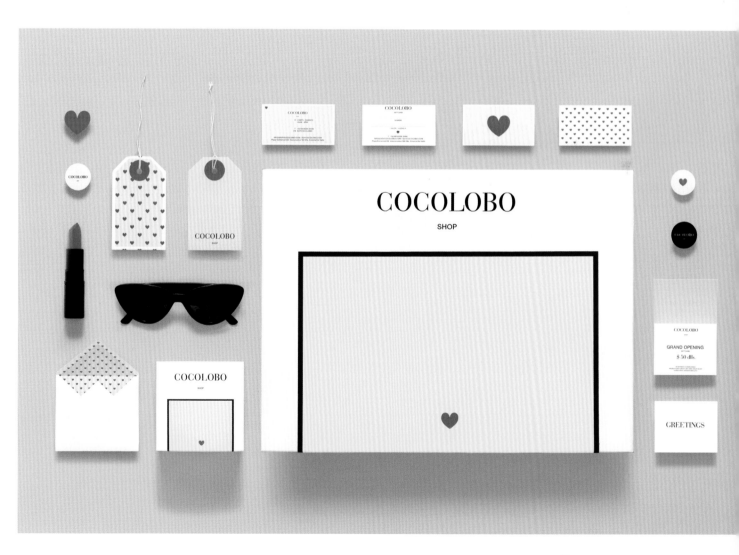

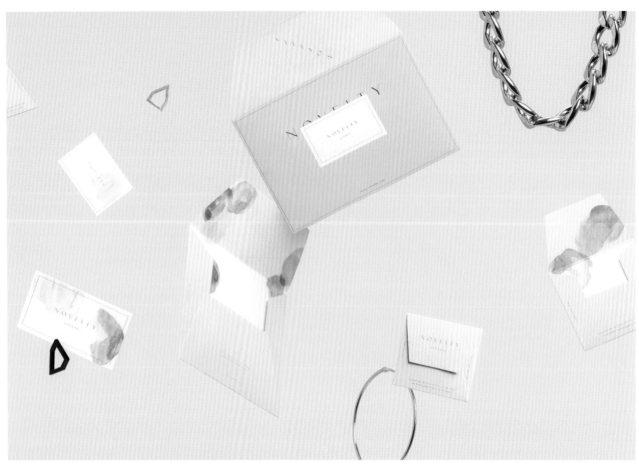

Novelty

Novelty is a shopping boutique that retails casual apparel to chic young women with a taste for fresh, modern fashion. The shop started up as a project by Novelty's partners once they returned from the exciting and ever-evolving New York fashion scene. The shop was to feature handpicked items that could be considered quirky and novel trendsetters, something you couldn't find in any other shop, hence Novelty became the name of the brand. Located in Calzada del Valle, a gardened boulevard inside the exclusive area of San Pedro, a suburb of the larger metropolitan city of Monterrey, Mexico. Novelty is the high-end fashion store of curiosity shops.

Design: Anagrama
Photography: Caroga Photographer (branding), Juma (shop interiors)

Grazia

Grazia is an eatery in Bogotá, Colombia where lovers of food can buy refined sweets and savory delicacies. The challenge of this project was to create a visual language that honors the beauty and perfection of the food. Design firm p576 began with a graphic investigation of the ingredient forms, which were later developed into a series of patterns for use on all the packing pieces. "We visited the local market with the chefs, picked some vegetables and fruits, and then went to their house to cut and to photograph the food," said Art Director Arutza Onzaga. She added, "we proposed a second brand element: lines that show the spatial structure of the objects and registers the logo position." These elements, along with the simplified typography, define the brand's sophisticated and modern style.

Design Agency: p576
Art Direction: Arutza Onzaga
Creative Direction: Arutza Onzaga
Design: Arutza Onzaga, María Silva
Photography: Max Morales, Ugo Passalacqua

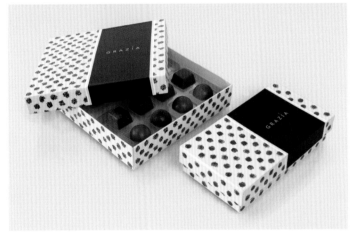

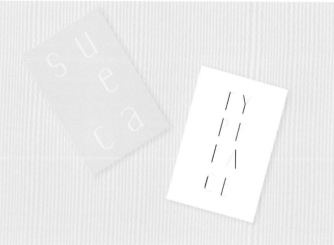

Sueca Typeface

Sueca was a typeface designed to emphasize the difference between thinness and thickness. Inspired by the simplicity and harmony of Swedish design, graphic designer Marta Vargas created this typeface after living in Sweden for a while. The light hues worked well with the typeface.

Design: Marta Vargas

Sense of Beauty

"Beauty without a scalpel" is the motto of the new beauty parlor Sense of Beauty in Graz. The owner Dr. Przemyslaw Strulak and his team are known for their soft and effective beauty and cosmetic treatments – all without the use of surgery and using modern technology and exclusive products. A particular aesthetic style was used in the corporate design to portray the subject of beauty in a warm, sensual and emotional way. The combination of the clear, simple black logo design and the peach-colored skin tone embodied professionalism and beauty.

Design Agency: moodley brand identity
Creative Direction: Mike Fuisz
Art Direction: Natascha Triebl
Design: Natascha Triebl

053

Frida von Fuchs

Frida von Fuchs is a Berlin-based company that writes concepts, develops ideas and coordinates campaigns together with freelance creatives. Designer Jono Garrett developed a character that is a hybrid of woman and fox, someone who looks out for you, but is never seen. For the application, Garrett imagined what their personal stationery might look like.

Design: Jono Garrett

Mecca Rebrand

Cosmetics Cubed is a multi brand cosmetics retailer based in Australia, including Mecca Cosmetica, Kit Cosmetics and Mecca Maxima. The old identity was out of date and the brief was to give it a refresh and possibly looking at grouping the sub brands under a new master name "Mecca brands." The new concept draws inspiration from the fact that Mecca is where beauty products from around the world come together exclusively in Australia. The identity is also quietly confident and draws on certain feminine cues.

Design: Sherman Chia J.W / Photography: Sherman Chia J.W

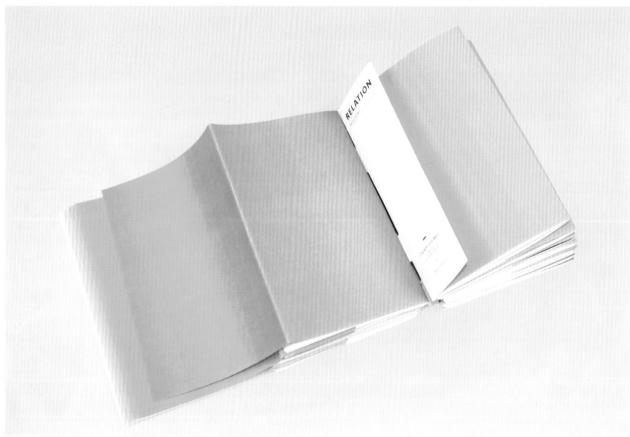

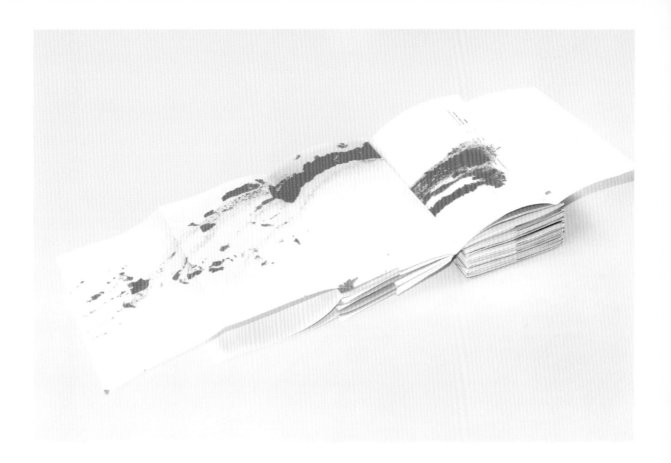

21 Words, 21 Works

The 21 Words, 21 Works project was designed around the exhibition "Graphic Design: Now in Production." Using five essays in the exhibition catalogue as the source material and crystallizing the content into one single word, the class investigated the themes and ideas of the show. Each of the 21 students was asked to contribute a 20-page signature towards this book based on the individual analysis and interpretation of the word they chose.

Design: Veronica Vespertine S.

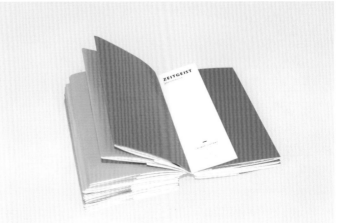

"The Me" Stationery Series

A piece of stationery is something personal and individual. The market place is over saturated with different types of stationery from illustrations to patterns and various graphics. The main objective of this concept series was to create a set of stationery pieces that was different and extremely personal. Each piece was hand painted with a special scratchy paint similar to those you would find on scratch cards. The key was that the plain stationery would reveal a unique pattern below. Thus each piece would be different depending on the user.

Design: Sherman Chia J.W
Photography: Sherman Chia J.W

BIG ME

MINI ME

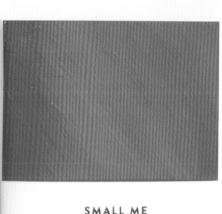

ME

SMALL ME

me
—nū

yummy kuchen

Schwarzwälder Kirschtorte	5
Erdbeerkuchen	3,5
Walnuss-Brownie	3,5
Schokodonut	2,5

today´s best

| Weiße Schokolade & Himbeere | 2 |
| Streuselkuchen mit Sahne | 4 |

to drink

Kaffe	2,5
Latte Macciato	3
Cappuccino	3
Chai Latte	3,5
Soft Drinks	2,5
Water (sparkling no sparkles)	2

cocktails

Tequilla Sunrise	8
Caipirinho	8
Mohito	8
Vokda/Jägermeister Redbull	8

EN—
JOY!

we are busy
—
yes, with eating
cookies!

coo—kie
berlin

please
clean our room
—
everywhere
are crumbles.

coo—kie
berlin

coo—kie
berlin

ere is your
—key

Welcome — at Cookie Hotel

coo—kie
berlin

Cookie Berlin
Alte Schönhauser
Straße 39
10178 Berlin
T. +49(0)30
512 312 0
F. +49(0)30
512 312 20
www.
cookies-berlin.de

hello

Cookie
Hotel Berlin

Fun and colorful, the corporate identity for the Cookie Hotel Berlin was created by two German graphic designers Deria Ormantzi and Sebastian Berbig. It's a typography-based and unconventional hotel brand identity with three different hues – bright red, pastel pink and fresh gold.

Design: Deria Ormantzi, Sebastian Berbig

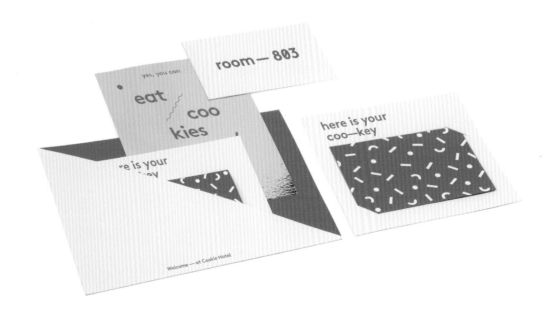

Jean Paul Gaultier

Jean Paul Gaultier was made as an application assignment for Beckmans College of Design. It was an assignment to make a poster and an invitation for the exhibition The Fashion World of Jean Paul Gaultier in Stockholm 2013.

Design: Anna Dormer Volgsten

Jackie Smith

Jackie Smith is a shoe & handbag brand that managed to position itself as one of Argentina's most important brands in the accessible luxury market. Taking the brand's name and its position in the market as starting points, design studio Estudio FBDI defined an identity that reflects the essence of a feminine world, classic, international, romantic, timeless and above all sophisticated. Inside this conceptual world the studio defined and designed Jackie's visual identity, logo, color palette, packaging and advertising campaigns. As a result of the brand's construction, Jackie Smith became, in only two collections, a top of mind brand within the handbags category.

Design: Estudio FBDI / Photography: Estudio FBDI

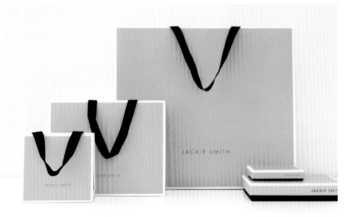

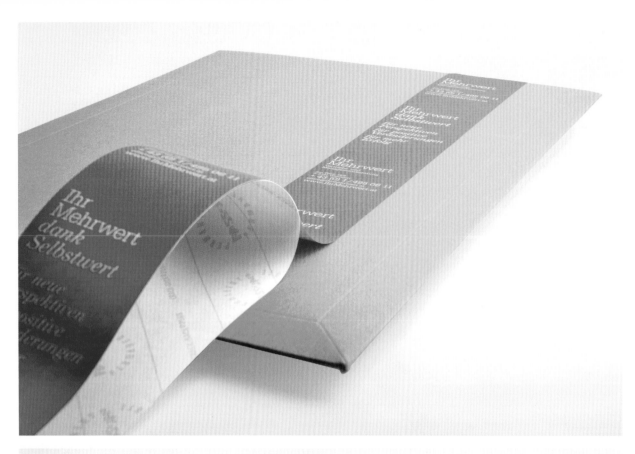

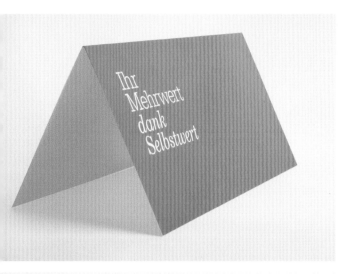

Ihr Mehrwert

Ihr Mehrwert ("Your Added Value") is a successful Austrian sales and management consulting company. The graphic design with the focus on colors emphasized its business concept: "Your added value due to self-value." The color sequence between red and magenta suggested openness, courage and eagerness to make decisions. At the same time, it provided space for intermediate steps. You might want to discover how much more there is behind "Ihr Mehrwert" as shown in the 3D tip effect of the business cards.

Design Agency: moodley brand identity
Design: Nora Obergeschwandner
Photography: Marion Luttenberger

Helvetica Hotel

Helvetica Hotel is not only a place to stay and relax, but also serves as a landmark that sells trend, culture and lifestyle that the typeface Helvetica generates. The essential theme of the branding was to propagate the visual attributes of the typeface, which are neutral, clean, and simple. While introducing typical hotel amenities in simplistic typography and color, the hotel also suggested a range of commercial items reinterpreted in 'Helvetica' way.

Design: Albert Son

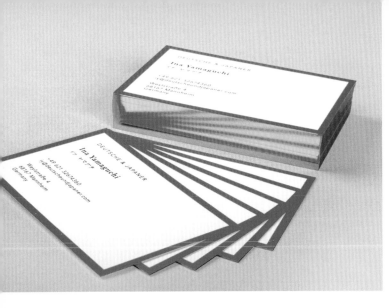

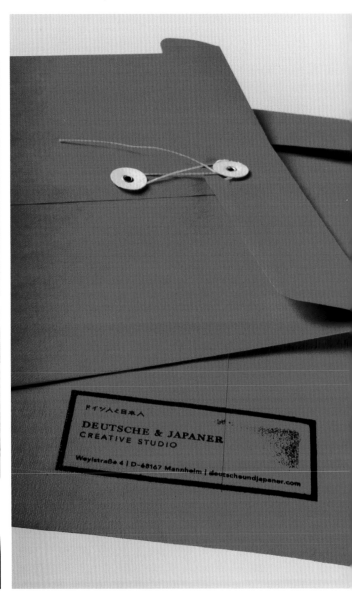

Deutsche & Japaner Corporate Design

The new printed materials for design studio Deutsche & Japaner, following the colors of Japanese and German national flags with the gold foil edges.

Design: Deutsche & Japaner

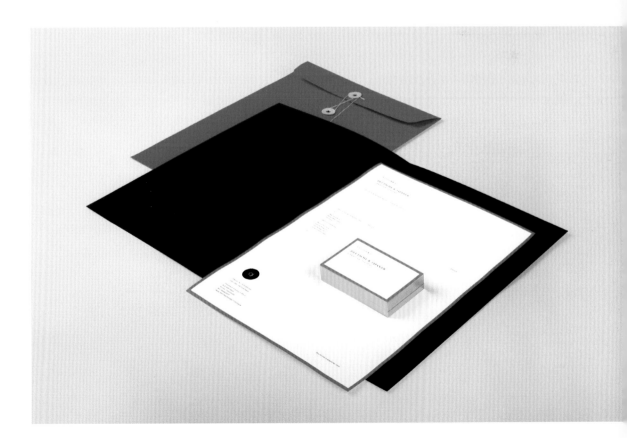

Fashion Walk Fashion Destination

Fashion Walk is a popular outdoor shopping area in Hong Kong. Design studio BLOW developed the key visuals with different collaterals and environmental graphics for their Fashion Walk Fashion Destination campaign to showcase the multitude of fashion and lifestyle brands that can be found in Fashion Walk.

Design Agency: BLOW / Design: Ken Lo

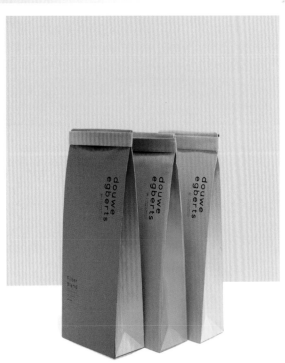

Douwe Egberts Rebrand

The aim of this project was to make Douwe Egberts into a brand that is more appealing to a younger audience and keeps it a premium brand recognized by its existing customers. Designer Sam Curtis gave the impression that this company is one of simple pleasures without complicate things and designs that overload you with information. Sometimes all you want is just a cup of coffee.

Design: Sam Curtis / Photography: Sam Curtis

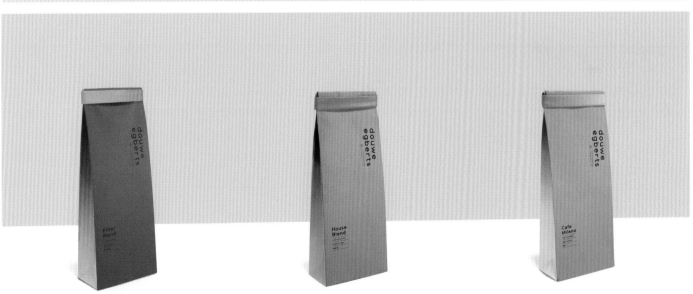

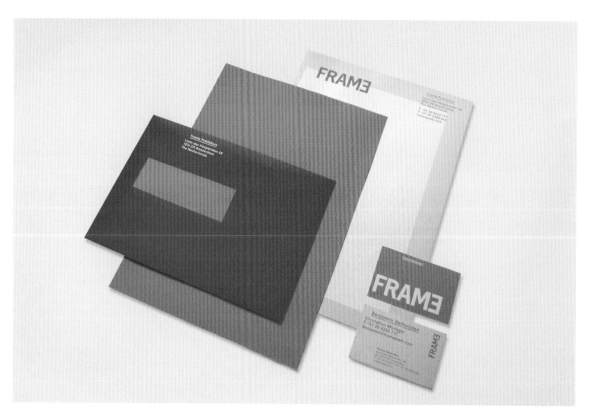

Frame Publishers

In-house designers Mariëlle van Genderen and Cathelijn Kruunenberg were commissioned to create a new visual identity for Frame Publishers. The new identity would be used in all corporate literature, business cards and its three major magazine titles – *Frame*, *Mark* and *Elephant*. Focusing on each of the three aspects as a unique entity, the designers assigned a different color for each title and this was then used as the core aspect of the design: pink for *Frame*, blue for *Mark* and green for *Elephant*.

Design Agency: Frame Publishers (Mariëlle van Genderen, Cathelijn Kruunenberg)

074

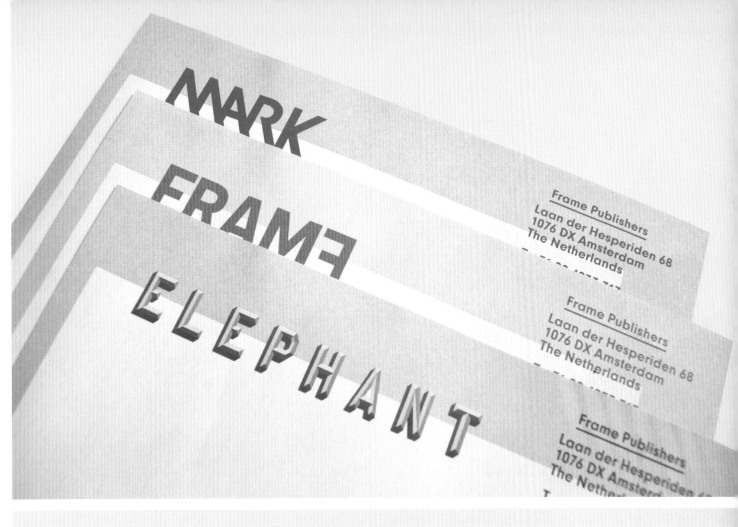

Tre Sekel

An collaboration with designer Emma Olbers, design agency
BrittonBritton was responsible for the overall strategy, branding and
product development concept for the new furniture brand Tre Sekel
(Three Centuries). As the name suggests, this collection rests on three
legs, anchored in three centuries. Sustainability in every aspect of the
expression is the main philosophy behind the Tre Sekel collection.

Design: BrittonBritton

076

House of Dagmar

Design agency BrittonBritton has been producing publications for House of Dagmar for quite some time. In the fall of 2012 they were asked work on their overall banding, image, and communication design. They took the challenge with exceptional care to create a stunning logo that matches the successful Swedish fashion brand.

Design: BrittonBritton

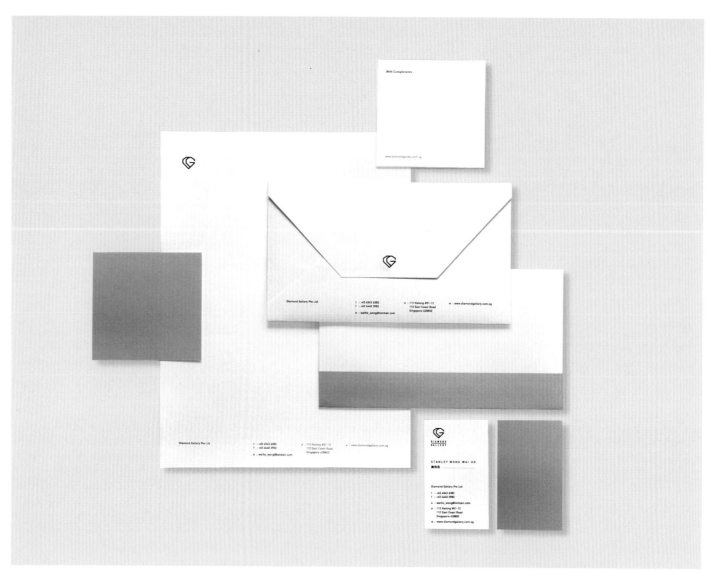

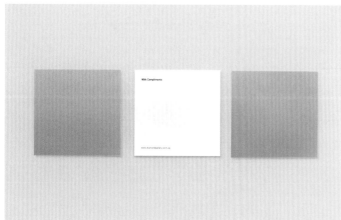

Diamond Gallery Brand Identity

Diamond Gallery's history in the diamonds, precious stones and jewelry line dates back to thirty years ago, where it started off as a diamond wholesale business in Hong Kong. This family-owned business officially opened its doors in Singapore in 2004. Design agency The Folks Studio refreshed the identity of this established brand so that it would appeal to the younger consumer. The brand colors – deep lilac and dusty gold, were chosen with care. When set in a gradient, it brings to mind the romantic first moments of dawn and last moments of dusk. This contemporary logo also draws inspiration from the Chinese saying " 好事成双 "or "good things come in pairs" – hence, the pair of diamonds.

Design Agency: The Folks Studio / Design: Yeo Zhengliang

Galerie Rodolphe Janssen

Galerie Rodolphe Janssen was founded in 1991 in Brussels and focuses on artists from Europe, Asia and America. The elegant logo and radial gradient (blue to white) were meticulously considered in order to obtain an exclusive result. The entire visual identity included logo, stationary, invitations, website (with content managing system), newsletter, etc.

Design Agency: Codefrisko / Design: Thomas Wyngaard

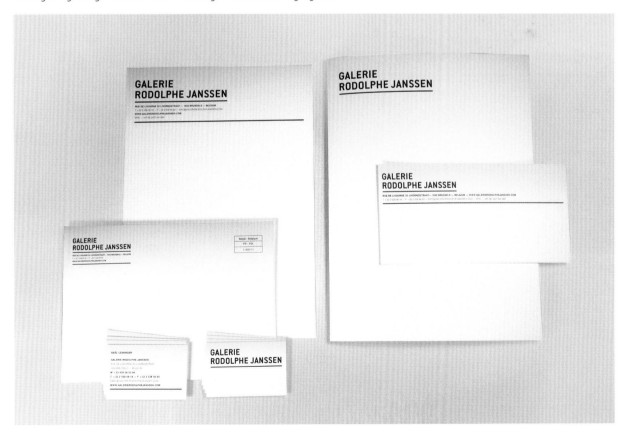

DOMINIC
REEVES

Furniture & Product Design

+44 (0) 7813 651894
dom@dominicreeves.co.uk
dominicreeves.co.uk

DOMINIC
REEVES

Furniture & Product Design

+44 (0) 7813 651894
dom@dominicreeves.co.uk
dominicreeves.co.uk

dominicreeves.co.uk

Dominic Reeves

Identity and stationery for an
independent furnuture and product
designer. The identity is inspired
by the story of Dr. Jekyll and Mr.
Hyde which is symbolic for the way
in which Dominic Reeves works.
Accordingly the letters in the logo
move into different directions.

Design: Mind Design

Bauwerk

Bauwerk creates exclusive property, ideally situated, where people can live peacefully, work and experience the bustle of the city. Class instead of mass! The corporate design developed by moodley brand identity lived up to this claim.

Design Agency: moodley brand identity / Creative Direction: Mike Fuisz
Art Direction: Alexandra Muralter / Design: Alexandra Muralter

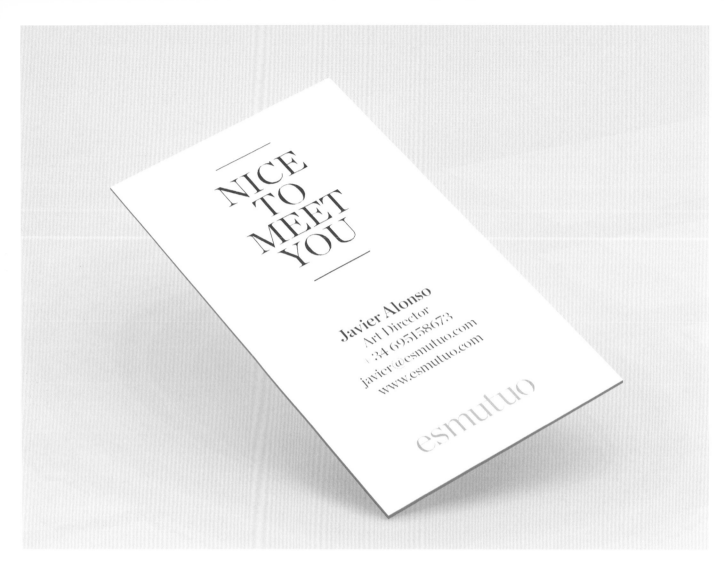

Esmutuo Branding

Branding and stationery for Esmutuo. Playing with a Mediterranean concept, soft, harmonious and pleasing appearance was used to introduce Esmutuo as a design studio.

Design: Esmutuo

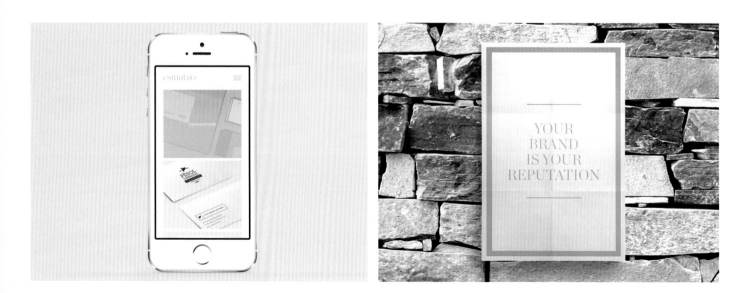

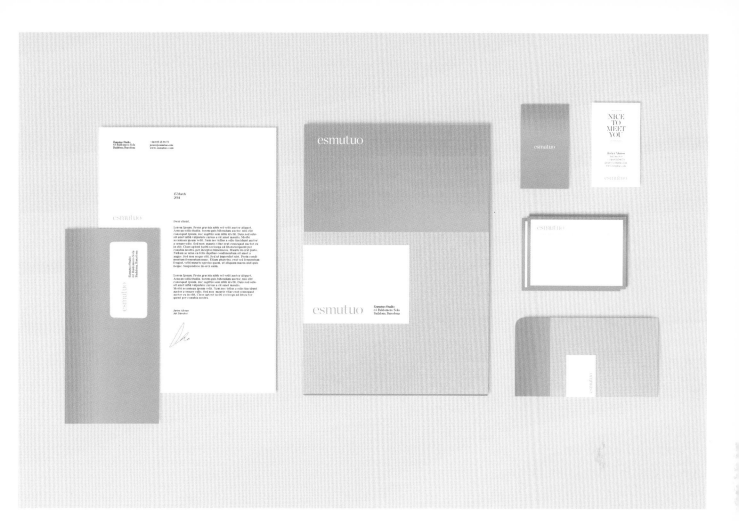

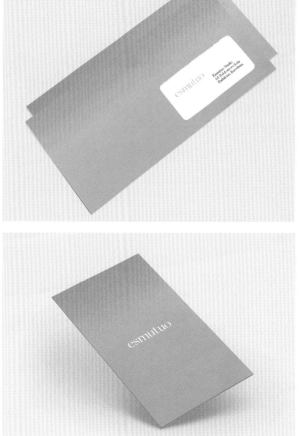

Talia Welka

Branding and identity for final year photographer, Talia Welka. The identity needed to be memorable, bold and elegant, creating a layer of professionalism and reliability in preparation for her degree show and post-college career. The concept revolves around a simple and logical design system – a pinhole.

Design: Abbas Mushtaq / Copywriter: Talia Welka
Photography: Talia Welka

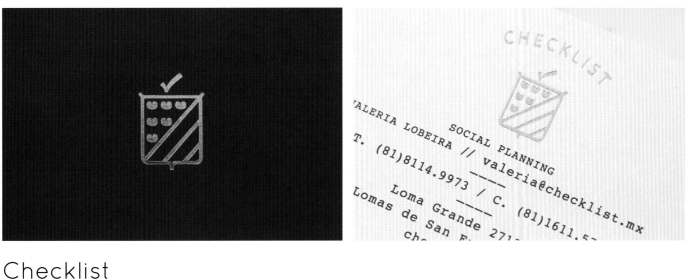

Checklist

Checklist specializes in custom event planning, especially for milestone occasions, such as birthdays, anniversaries, graduations, holiday parties and corporate events. Their services are custom, catered exclusively for each client's unique needs and always aim towards sweet perfection.

This design proposal gave Checklist an institutional look (proper of a university or college) with a jovial color palette. The combination was meant to convey commitment and trustworthiness, but with a youthful feminine touch that ensured that every detail was never overlooked but always cared for. The pastel colors were gentle, cozy and soothing, the deep blue serious and convincing. The type selection, reminiscent of 1950's secretarial typewriting, went hand in hand with the conservatory institutional and feminine attention to detail concept.

Design: Anagrama / Photography: Caroga Photographer

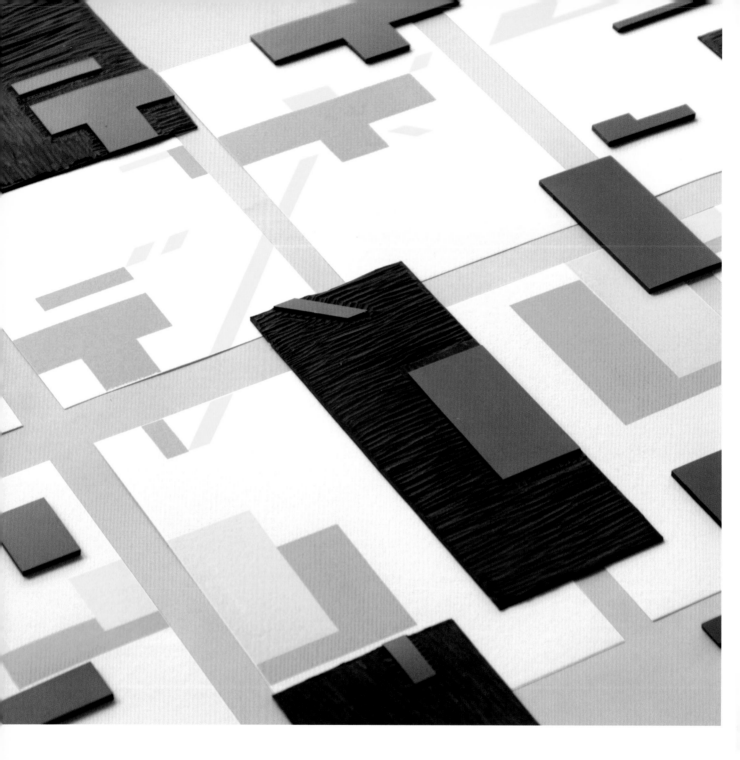

Decoboco

This work was exhibited at the exhibition of letterpress. The rubber plate for prints was carved by hand.

Design Agency: smbetsmb / Design: Keita Shimbo, Misaco Shimbo

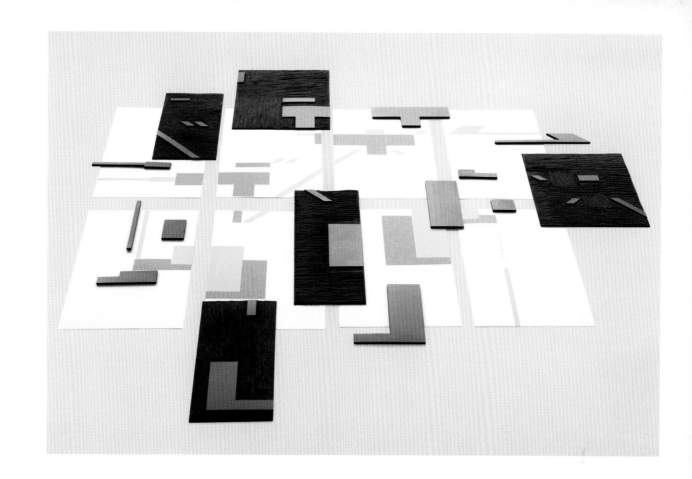

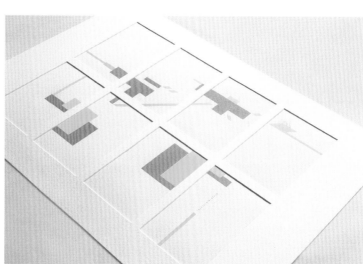

Proportion
8515

This project was a part
of the Graphic Design
Walk 2012 exhibition held
in conjunction with the
London Design Festival.
Working along the theme
of PROPORTION, this
was a graphical and
typographical expression
of the ratio of men to
women designers in
the design industry. The
proportions of the graphics
& type were based on the
85:15 proportion.

Design Agency: Foreign
Policy Design Group
Design: Yah-Leng Yu

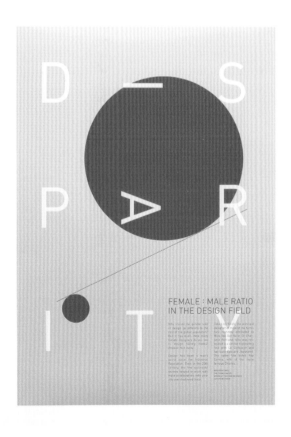

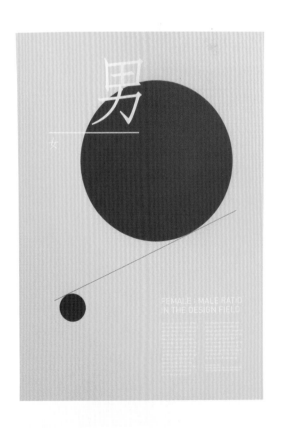

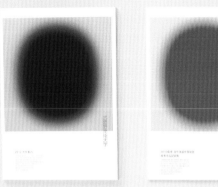
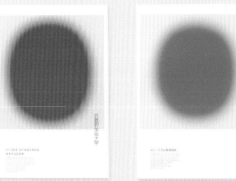

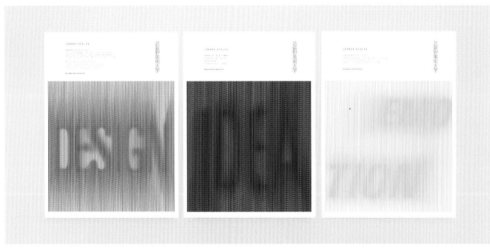

Musashino Art University 2012 & 2014

Art direction for Musashino Art University 2012 & 2014. With the aim of emphasizing the role of the art university as a venue for creative activity, the message was condensed into the beauty of color.

Art Direction: Daigo Daikoku
Design: Daigo Daikoku, Takao Minamidate
Photography: Akitada Hamasaki

CEE – Coalition for Engaged Education

CEE is an organization in LA that stands for the right of society's most vulnerable youth to realize their potential through education that ignites and inspires them. Founded by Dr. Paul Cummins, a celebrated educator, the organization needed a new identity to signal their intent to broaden their mission. The logo is both wordmark and icon. It joyfully reflects CEE's process of transforming and uplifting as well as the extraordinary system of support they give their students throughout their journeys. CEE was turned into a verb to let people know the organization's beliefs and the students' own hopes and dreams.

Design Agency: Blok Design
Creative Direction: Vanessa Eckstein, Marta Cutler
Design: Vanessa Eckstein, Kevin Boothe
Copywriter: Marta Cutler

Bassetti Home Innovation Stores Identity

Bassetti is an historical Italian brand that retails home textile. Designer La Tigre and Gianluca Seta were commissioned to redesign the brand's identity. Starting from a given logo, the proposal came from the idea that Bassetti expresses the concepts of light and day, game and functionality. The colorful gradient conveyed an unexpected energy in contrast with the plain white.

Design: La Tigre, Gianluca Seta / Photography: Matteo Cremonini

Vintage and Cofee

An identity representing the key values of the brand was created and particularly reflected through the naming and slogan. Fresh and vivid colors showed a world full of new sensations and tastes.

Design Agency: Masquespacio
Design: Ana Milena Hernández Palacios
Photography: David Rodríguez Pastor

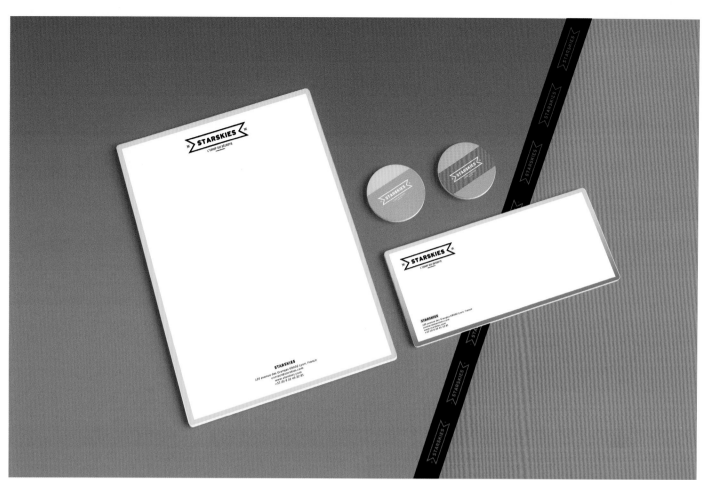

Starskies

Starskies was a French concept store with posters and postcards. Its aim was to express joy, fun, and a furtive desire to return to childhood. Bright and neon colors were the local point of the visual identity. These colors provided strength and dynamism. Each creation was treated in a minimalistic and colorful way with a quirky wink and a slight retro touch. Starskies was an ingenious decoration project where typefaces and images were mixed with a touch of whim.

Design Agency: B&T Studio / Design: Blandine Tracol / Photography: Blandine Tracol

Middle of Nowhere

Identity and collateral re-design for boutique Australian wall art and home décor brand Middle of Nowhere. The identity was designed to be neutral, and change in color to reflect the items and collections it appears with, keeping the identity playful and fashionable, ensuring it becomes an integral part of the ever-evolving product range.

Design Agency: Mildred & Duck / Design: Daniel Smith, Sigiriya Brown
Photography: Jon Ong, Kristian van der Beek

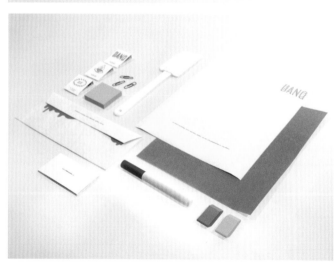

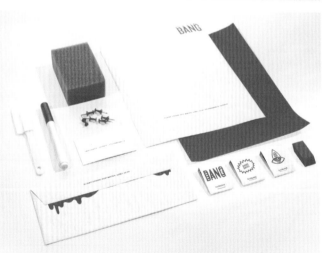

Atelier BangBang

Atelier BangBang was the result of the final studies project of UQAM graphic design B.A.. Designer Simon Laliberte wanted to improve the branding of a screen-printing workshop and provide this company a set of products, articles and promotional items of all kinds. The workshop was born in February 2012. BangBang is not only a screen-printing workshop for paper and textile but also a design studio and an experimentation lab. The workshop is set to be a reference in terms of screen-printing and design in Montreal, aspiring to work with a mixed clientele and offer high quality service.

Design: Simon Laliberte

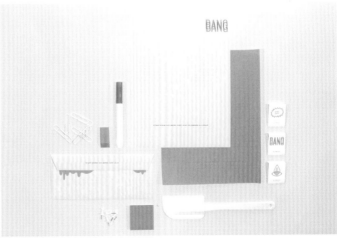

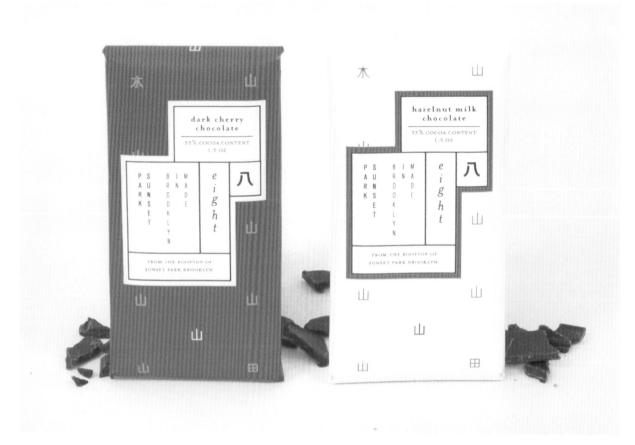

Eight Rooftop Garden

This was a packaging project for a Brooklyn based rooftop garden called Eight. This garden is based in Sunset Park, Brooklyn which is a neighborhood made up of immigrants of Chinese decent. The garden is named after the number 8, which is known as a symbol for wealth and prosperity in Chinese culture. The neighborhood lies not-so-coincidentally on 8th Avenue in Brooklyn.

The design language was inspired by Chinese calligraphy, which valued the balance of order and dynamism. It also used the direction of writing and reading in old Chinese scripts – top to bottom, right to left.

The patterns were inspired by the region where the majority of the immigrants were from Fujian, China, which was made up of primarily mountainous areas. Chinese characters for mountain, water and fields were also used to bring forward the geography of the region.

Design: Esther Li

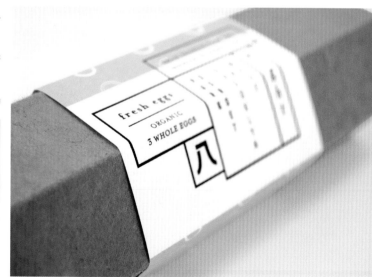

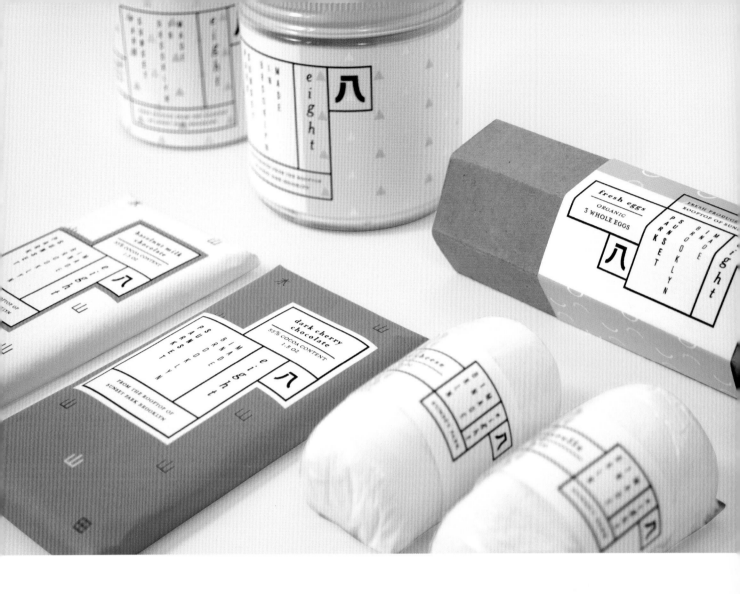

El Aristo®

Design agency Empatia® was asked to design the visual identity and packaging of a tea's house based in Jujuy, Argentina. El Aristo® sells high level tea. Tea is the second most consumed beverage on Earth after water, and in many cultures it is also consumed at elevated social events, such as afternoon tea and tea party. Afternoon tea or low tea is a small meal snack typically eaten between 4 pm and 6 pm. Observance of the custom originated amongst the wealthy classes in England in the 1840s.

Recreating the personality of the brand, Empatia® developed a new colorful system, where the products could be combined with modern and powerfull colors and elements. Empatia® synthesized the logo, making it more appealing and modern.

Design: Empatia®

102

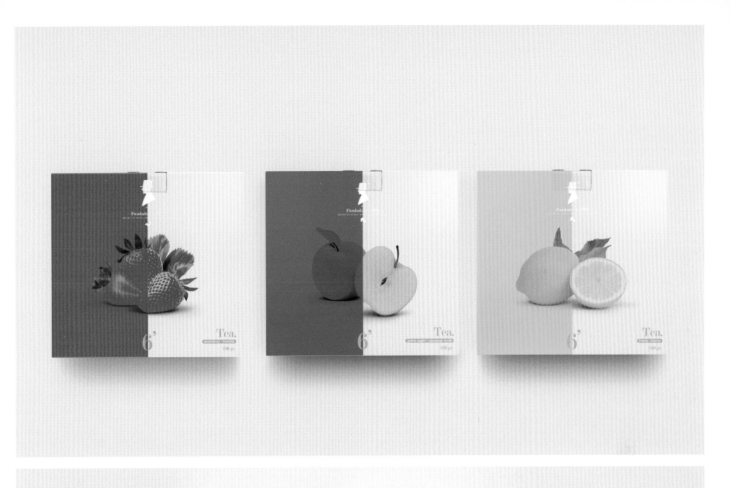

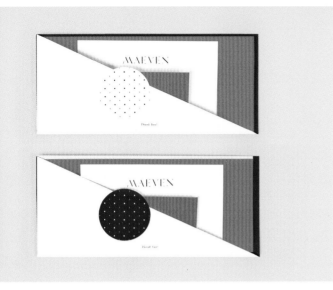

Maeven

Identity for Maeven (pronounced may-ven), a Brooklyn-based online shop with a collection of vintage and preowned designer clothing. The pattern, used in packaging materials ranging from tissue paper to stickers and mailing bags, uses the two thicknesses of the logo to form a texture reminiscent of pixels, referring to the vintage shop operating online. The colors are a modern interpretation of the vintage red and blue striped envelopes.

Design: Lotta Nieminen

Idep Barcelona

IDEP Barcelona is one of the best design schools in Barcelona. They commissioned Design agency Querida Studio to develop their new visual identity. Querida Studio came to the conclusion that a flexible identity was the best solution to their needs, which might be initially more expensive than static identities, but can save a lot of money in the long run.

Design Agency: Querida Studio
Design: Marc Sancho

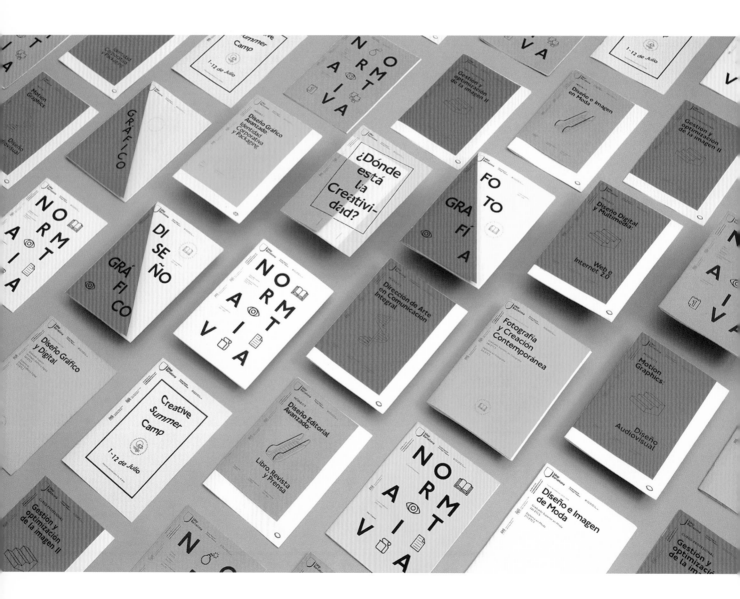

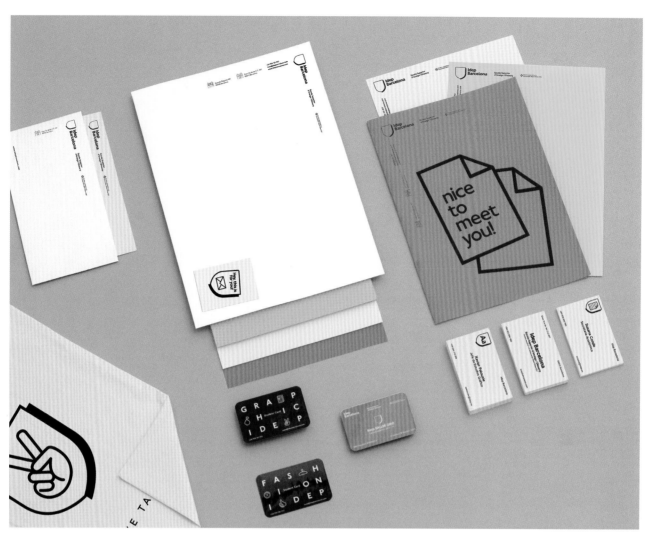

Piper & Sons

Piper & Sons is a children's clothing and accessories line for kids ages 0 to 5. The branding for Piper & Sons is characterized by a cool, contemporary style, high brand value, and exceptional craftsmanship. Drawing inspiration from nature, fantasy, and the youthful innocence of children, the proposal consists of a mature logotype that communicates the brand's premium value and a whimsical jumping fox reminiscent of typical children's fairy tale characters. The fox illustration was carefully crafted by hand, making sure its illustrative detail was fuzzy, friendly, cute and, at the same time, contemporary and young. The color palette features mint, a choice color that provides a cool, youthful and natural pop to each piece that is appealing to both girls and boys. The copper foil print finished over uncoated paper is thrown in to round up the brand's whimsy and subtly elegant characteristics.

Design: Anagrama
Photography: Caroga Photographer

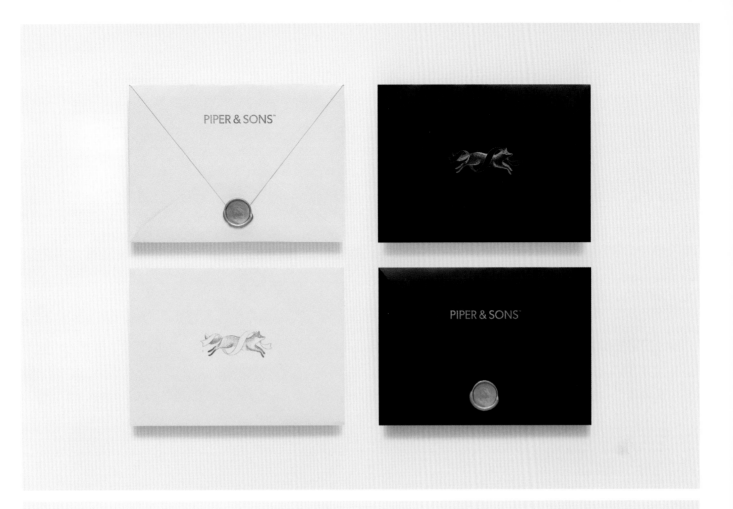

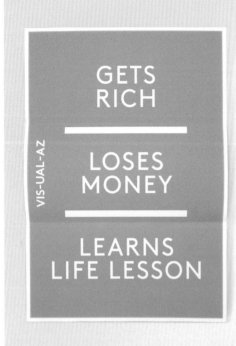

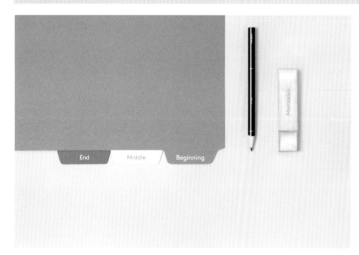

Visualaz

Visualaz, a film and production studio, specializes in short films for weddings and corporate clients. In repositioning the company for a more discerning audience, there was an opportunity to connect through storytelling – practicing what they preach to their clients. Every great story has a beginning, middle and end. This was the starting point for a playful visual and verbal identity, based on the three-part story structure. The name lent itself perfectly to this, helping the pronunciation through a phonetic structure. Each piece tells its own story to create a memorable experience.

Design Agency: RE / Creative Direction: Jason Little
Art Direction: Alex Creamer / Copywriter: Alex Creamer, Jason Little

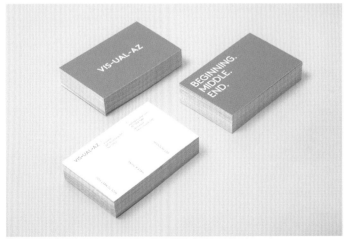

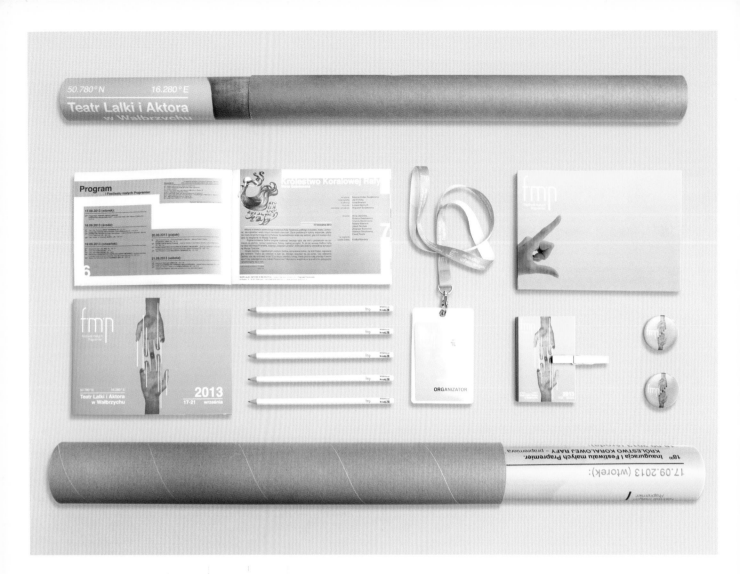

Festiwal małych Prapremier

Festiwal małych Prapremier was a nationwide Polish puppet festival, organized by the Puppet Theater in Wałbrzych. The most interesting preview shows for children/youth and modern dramaturgy readings have been performed during the event. The festival became the platform for integration of artist communities and audience through various meetings and panel discussions. The FmP has united almost the whole community of puppeteers. Beginning with theatre managers and ending with playwrights, it definitely came as a great success. The main idea for this project was to avoid the infantile character that accompanies most of the similar festivals. Minimalist form, ascetic typography and metaphorical theme of the animator helped mix form and functions, both informative and image-building.

Creative Direction: Marcin Szmidt
Art Direction: Marcin Szmidt, Monika Domagała
Design: Marcin Szmidt
Copywriter: Marlena Jasińska-Denst

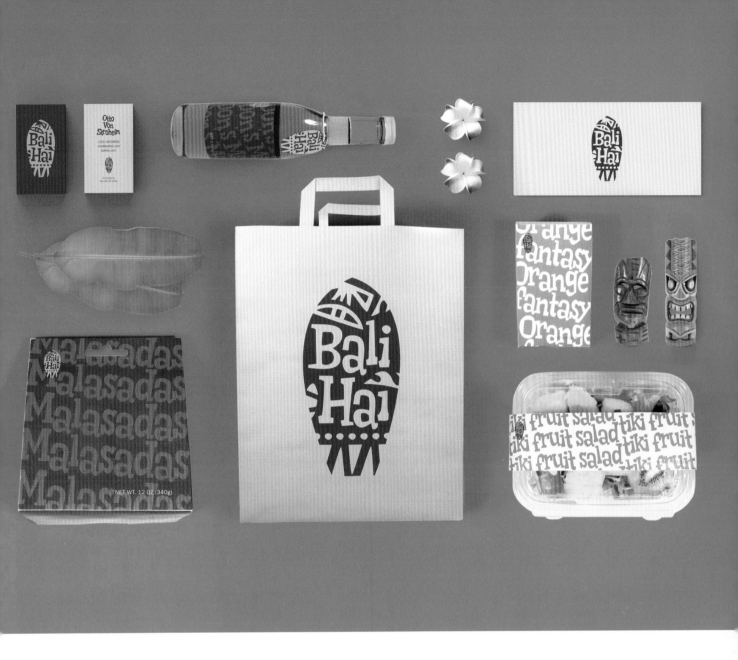

Bali Hai Food Market

Bali Hai is a Hawaiian food market in New York City. The key element of the branding is to create a tangible and accessible Hawaiian hotspot in New York City that offers moods of exotic Tiki culture to visitors. This is achieved by creating a playful, vibrant, and authentic Hawaiian environment with bright colors and patterns of traditional Tiki masks incorporated throughout.

Design: Albert Son

7-Eleven Coffee Concept Sweden

By updating the design of the coffee concept, Swedish 7-Eleven wanted to change customer perceptions towards the more modern and urban. The coffee experience is characterized by speed and easy access, and a sense of micro pause.
Choices of colors, materials and details were made to balance a quick buying process with a comfortable coffee break. Communication and signage were designed to enable easy as well as inspiring way finding and product selection. Cups, bags and packaging were developed where the iconic stripes have been used as starting points for treatments of each identity carrier.

Design: BVD

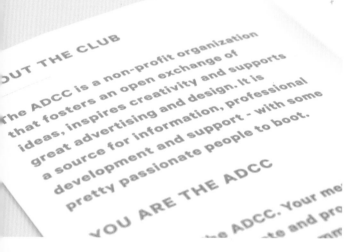

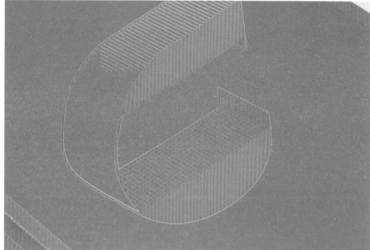

ADCC

The Advertising and Design Club of Canada needed to drive membership. Design agency Blok Design worked to add greater, more robust benefits for its members and created this provocative piece designed to communicate the advantages and prestige of belonging to such an august community of like-minded thinkers and creators.

Design Agency: Blok Design / Creative Direction: Vanessa Eckstein, Marta Cutler
Design: Vanessa Eckstein, Patricia Kleeberg / Copywriter: Marta Cutler

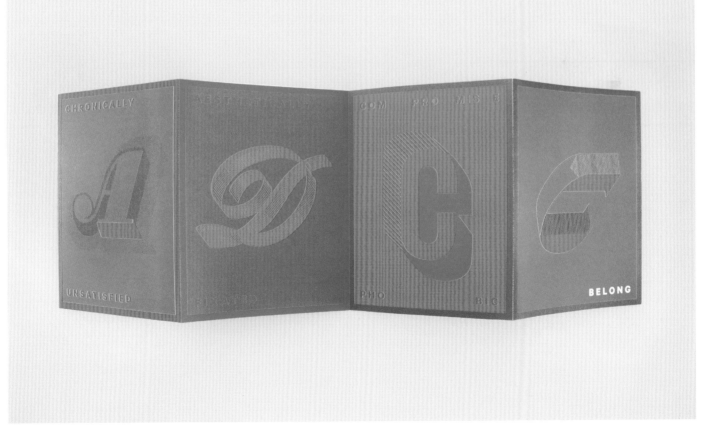

Carté

Carté is a social stationary boutique that offers custom-made printed material for all kinds of social events. Carté started as a small business that has grown larger throughout the years. They wanted to rebrand themselves with an identity that reflects the high quality of their work as well as their focus in excellent customer service.

The identity is inspired by the hand-made production methods that Carté uses to create their printed pieces, and their hands-on approach of fulfilling the customer's wishes. The colors were selected because of the way they balance and compliment each other, appealing to the large feminine market without neglecting the male customer market.

Design Agency: Firmalt / Creative Direction: Manuel Llaguno / Art Direction: Francisco Puente
Design: Manuel Llaguno / Photography: Daniela Barocio

Essentials

Design agency PalauGea designed Fedrigoni's catalog Essentials – eight booklets showing different special papers for design projects, packaging, editorial, branding, etc. Stored in a black case, each booklet has a different cover design in order to classify and identify different type of paper.

Design: PalauGea

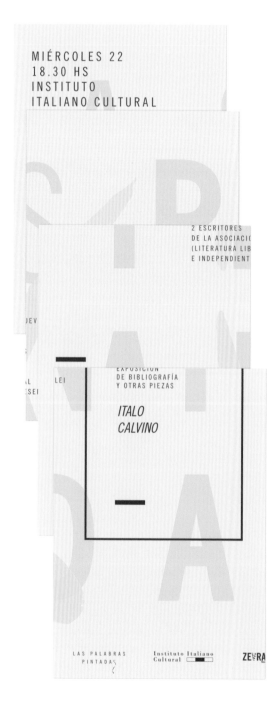

Las Palabras Pintadas

Las Palabras Pintadas was an academic project done for a design subject, serving as the visual identity of a literature work of Italo Calvino in an independent cultural centre in the city of Buenos Aires. The mixture of colors generates a surreal and confusing feeling typical of the author's fantasy. "I have enjoyed this project very much due to the fact that I love literature and I have found the experimentation of contrasting colors really interesting when it is given a neon effect," said designer Lucía Izco.

Design: Lucía Izco

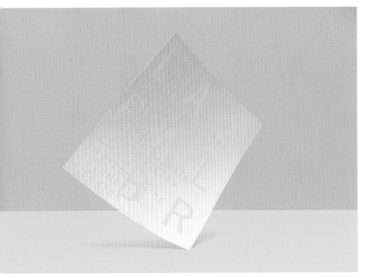

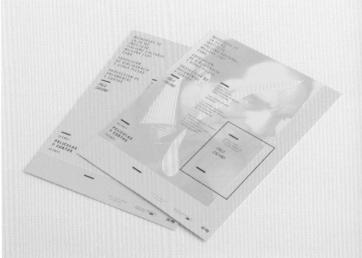

122

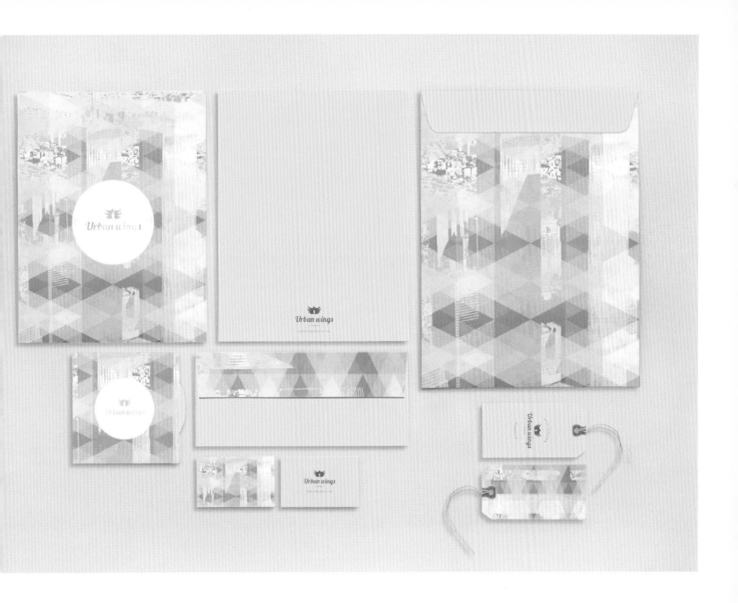

Urban Wings

Exclusively created in digital printing, Urban Wings is a youth brand for bedding and decoration, made in 2013 for the collection of Texathenea, the company designer Alessia Antonaci is currently working for. The designer developed the brand as a whole from logo design and corporate identity to the patterns for textile applications. The design features four different variants of color: turquoise, pink, bourdeaux, blue. Urban Wings is for young and modern people.

Design: Alessia Antonaci
Copywriter: Texathenea S.L.

Strata Bakery

Strata Bakery is a homemade pastries bakery. The identity idea, "Layers," is based on the analysis of the way the bakery's cakes are constructed with multiple layers of ingredients. Starting from the layer concept as a graphic synthesis of the product, design studio P·A·R adapted it to the different applications using different resources and reinforced the graphic image with a striking chromatic range that contrasts with the variety of materials and baked goods.

Design: P·A·R

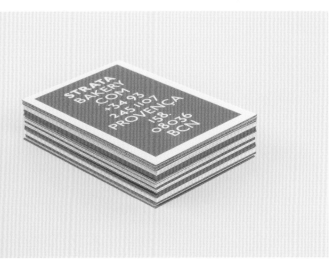

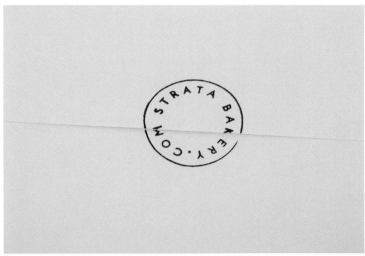

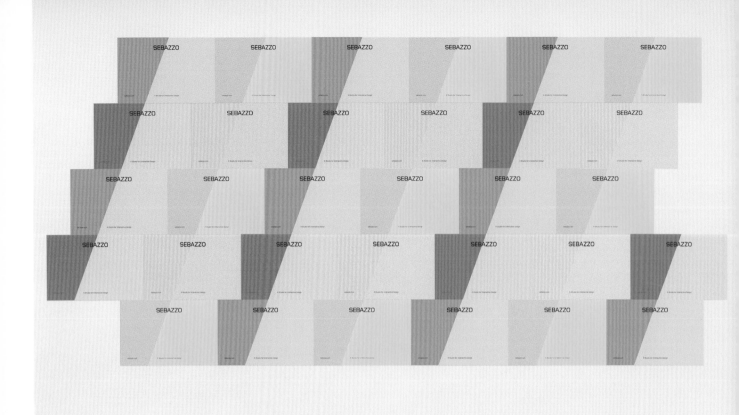

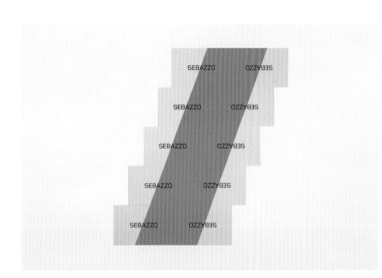

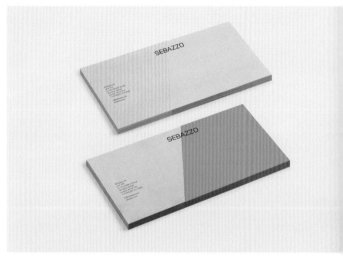

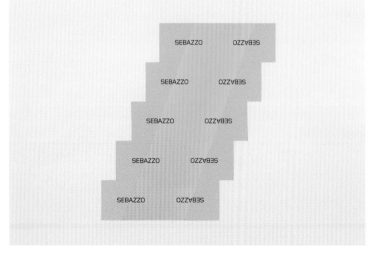

Sebazzo

Constructed from Gridnik – the logotype's uppercase sans-serif letterforms, 45-degree corners, monoline weight, structure and geometry, as well as its compounded nature, all point towards a straightforward and confident technological efficiency and neatly reference the designers that make up Sebazzo. The diagonal cut of the bright and pastel boards that make up the business cards create a striking but restrained dual tone and subtle dynamic aesthetic that feels like a simple but effective distillation of a two-man studio which compliments the ideation of the name and neatly splits the logotype into its two constituent parts. These are neatly unified by the tactile and crafted qualities of their paper marquetry construction.

Design Agency: Bunch / Creative Direction: Denis Kovac
Printer: Cerovski / Copywriter: Richard Baird

SANO Juice

SANO is a Barcelona-based juice and smoothie bar specializing in healthy and natural food – salads, wraps and daily menus. The complete redesign of the brand offered a fresher look, using the colors of the fruits to create beautiful graphic elements and explain the product as easy as possible. The project included the design of menus, flyers, basic stationery and some packaging elements.

Creative Direction: Marina Soto / Design: Marina Soto
Illustration: Kevin Sabariego

Personal Stationery

Personal stationery to promote Daniel Renda's design services. Minimal and eye catching, the stationery set includes business cards, letterheads and envelopes. Designer Daniel Renda selected three visually stimulating swatches of similar value and paired them with a grotesk typeface. The "slash" element switches color throughout the design to add variety while staying consistent. All the stationery was letterpress printed on a Vandercook letterpress by Naomie Ross and Daniel Renda. As a final touch the designer chose to paint the edges of each set of business cards to match the color of the corresponding "slash" element.

Design: Daniel Renda / Photography: Daniel Renda

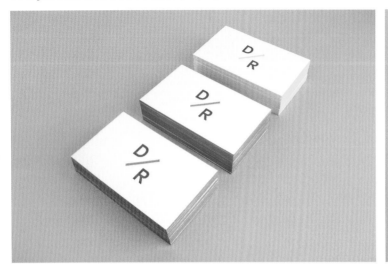

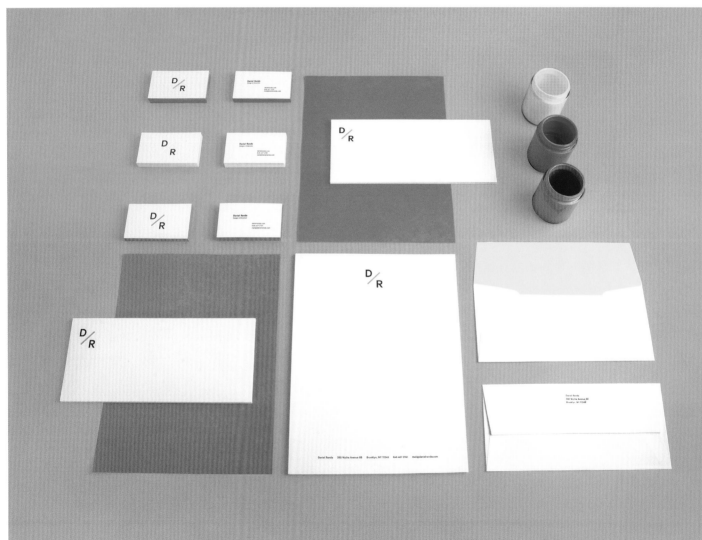

Cokoc Grill Take Away Restaurants

Cokoc Grill is a take-away restaurant with gourmet style where the farm chicken is the main meal. Its architecture and interior design is inspired by the ecological country life in an urban context. The wood, the vintage tile, the slate and the wicker items conceptualize the wellness and simplicity of the natural. With touches of color in packaging and urban typography that enhances the feedback between the countryside and the city, the take-away products are in recycled textures and simplified design.

Design: MABAA™ / Photography: MABAA™, Cokoc Grill

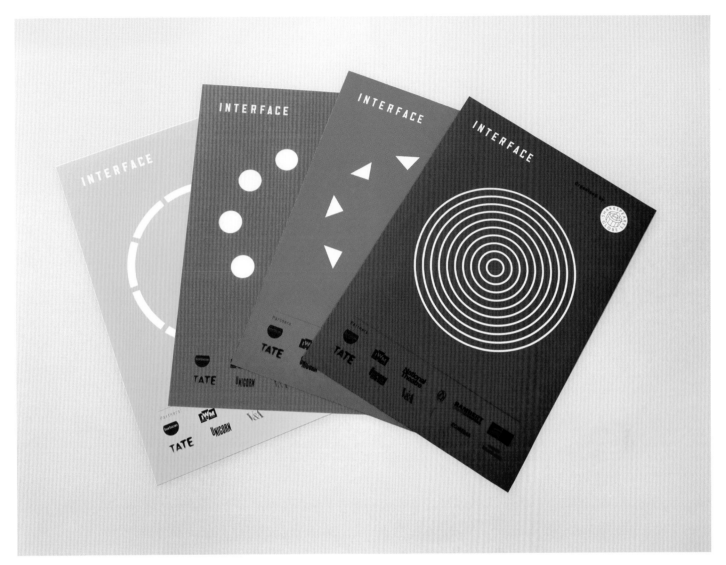

Shakespeare's Globe's Interface

Identity design for Shakespeare's Globe's first digital networking event, Interface. The event brought together ten of London's leading cultural institutes with 40 new digital agencies. The design featured 4 circular motifs, separated into ten pieces to represent the guests. Each of the circles connected, flowing into one another as a reference to the nature of networking.

Design: Patrick Fry

134

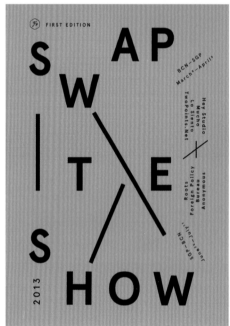

The Swap Show

The Swap Show is an exhibition exchange between design studios and creative agencies from cities around the world designed to showcase and celebrate creative work internationally. Stretching beyond material exchanges, The Swap Show provides an experience and raises design awareness across the board. It calls for good design, perspectives and people to congregate, because sharing is good. The Swap Show logo allows for various permutations – all of which form meanings that align with The Swap Show's identity of creative exchange and interaction.

Design Agency: Foreign Policy Design Group
Creative Direction: Yah-Leng Yu
Art Direction: Yah-Leng Yu
Design: Yah-Leng Yu, Liquan Liew, Judith Lee

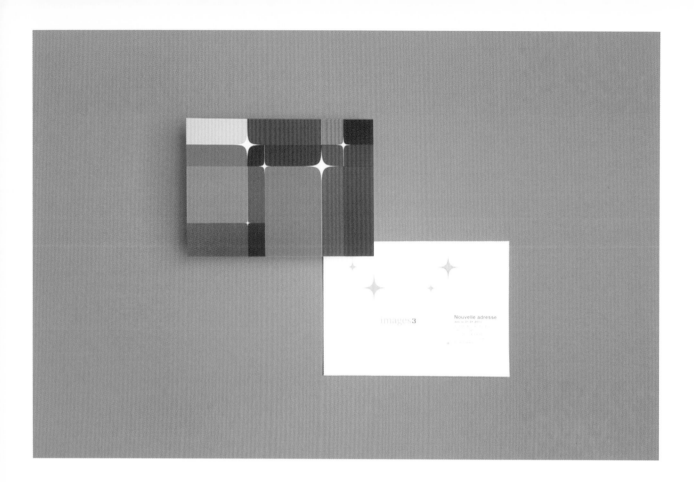

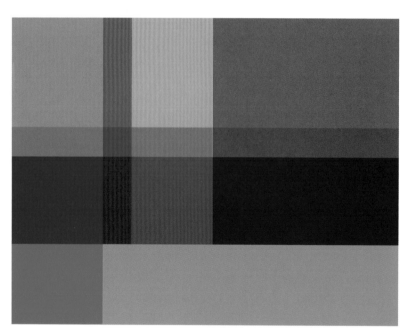

Images3 Corporate Identity

The colored shapes illustrate the core activity of Images3 specializing in prepress and image retouching. Images3 works in the heart of the image where pixels become artwork.

Design Agency: Enzed
Design: Mélanie and Nicolas Zentner

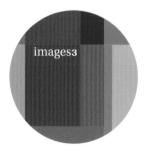
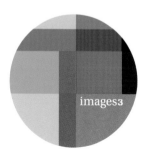
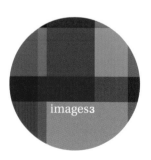
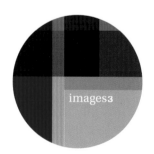

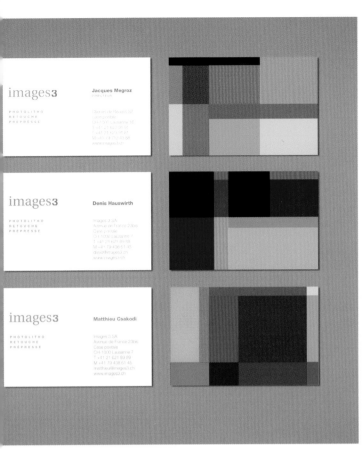

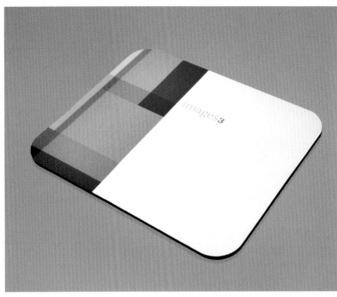

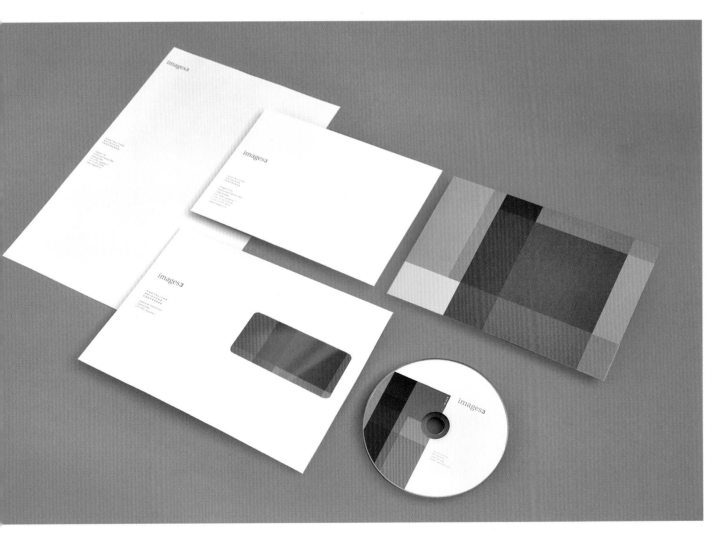

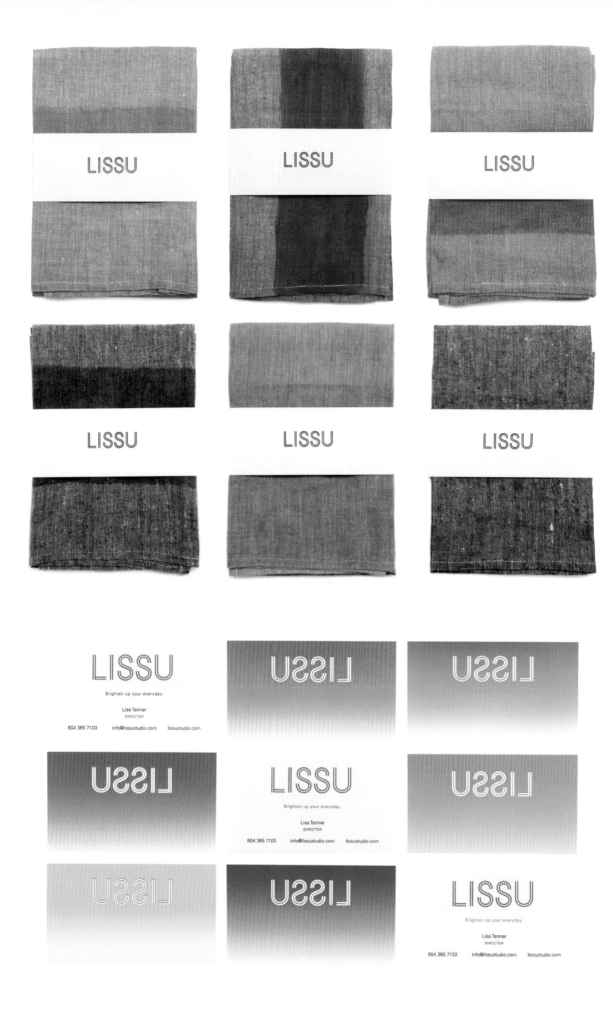

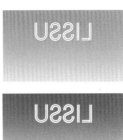

Lissu

Lissu is a range of individually hand-painted products and made from 100% European linen. Designed by Lisa Tanner, they are inspired by Scandinavia's fondness for functional simplicity and bold color. Lissu's products are designed to become your lifelong companions. Design studio Glasfurd & Walker worked with Lissu to create the brand identity applied to stationery, product packaging and brand material. On product packaging and stationery the logo was laser cut out of paper to allow the color and texture of the product to shine through.

Design: Glasfurd & Walker

Ontour On Strike

For the lookbook of On Strike Autumn/Winter 2011 Collection, the question was to create images that capture the spirit of their collection that is inspired by activists' protests and underground resistance. For the photoshoot a set of multicolored and abstract signboards were created. These accompanied the models and were used to incorporate in the lookbook of the collection. Design studio Raw Color did the photoshoot of the campaign and products as well as the design of the lookbook.

Ontour is a contemporary label driven by creativity. Ontour products reflect a sophisticated style with a recognizable twist. Subtle detailing, materials and use of color are a translation of Raw Color's passion for graphic and product design. Every season the collection is based upon a journey, inspired by daily life.

Design: Raw Color / Photography: Raw Color

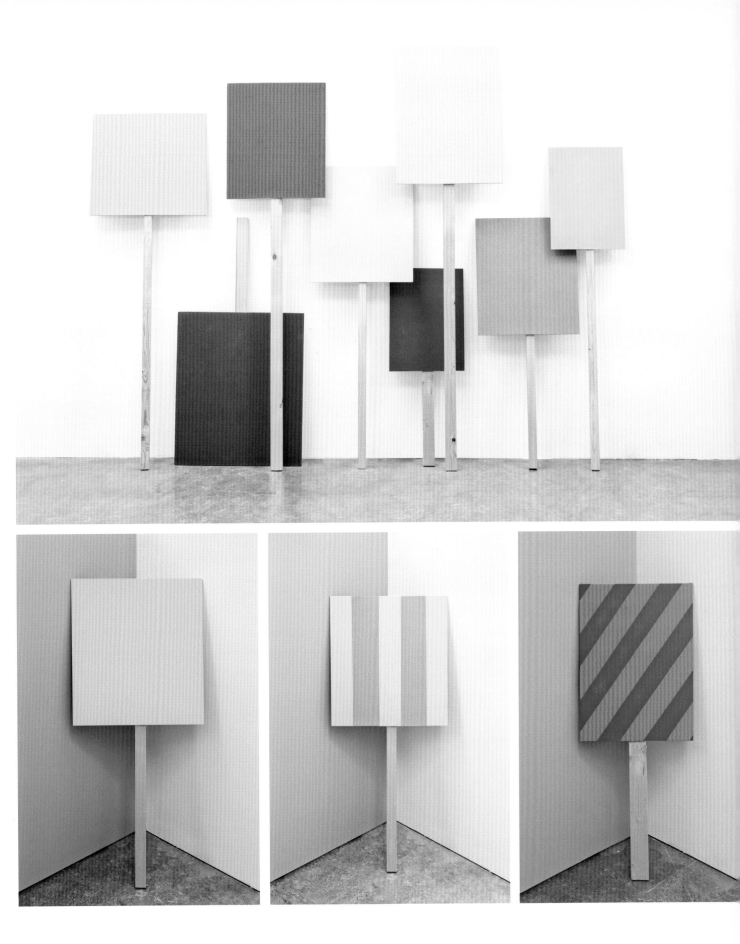

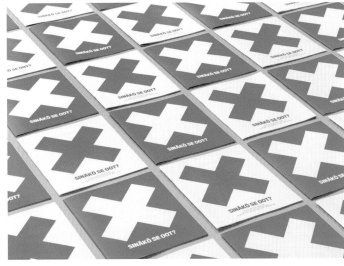
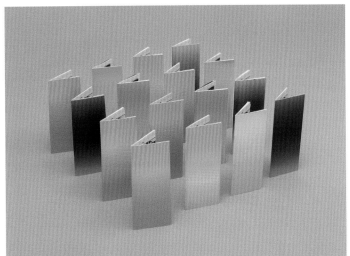

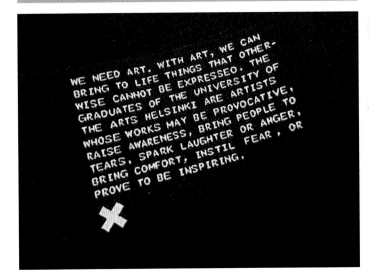
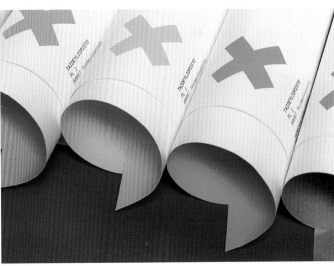

Branding of University of the Arts Helsinki

In the beginning of 2013, the Finnish Academy of Fine Arts, Sibelius Academy and Theatre Academy Helsinki merged into University of the Arts Helsinki. Design agency Bond provided the new top university with a complete branding solution. At the core of the visual identity is a simple and bold 'X' symbol that connects the top-level university brand with the three academy brands. The symbol is as rich with meaning as art itself: a starting point, a destination, a meeting place, a location, a signature, an unknown force, a warning, an irritant, a question, a solution.

Design Agency: Bond Creative Agency / Creative Direction: Arttu Salovaara
Design: Jesper Bange, James Zambra, Toni Hurme / Production: Mirva Kaitila
Photography: Mikko Ryhanen, Paavo Lehtonen, Veikko Kahkonen

Hornhuset

Hornhuset is like a bustling little square somewhere around the Mediterranean. A melting pot on three floors for those who want to enjoy a menu of flavorful, smaller dishes, or buy exceptionally tasty takeout. Hornhuset is a mix of all the good things from around the mediterranean and that is what should be expressed in the identity. Fresh bold colors, a playful typography and frame bind it together. All with a sun bleached feeling of summer.

Design Agency: Planet Creative
Design: Thomas Andersson, Tobias Ottomar

146

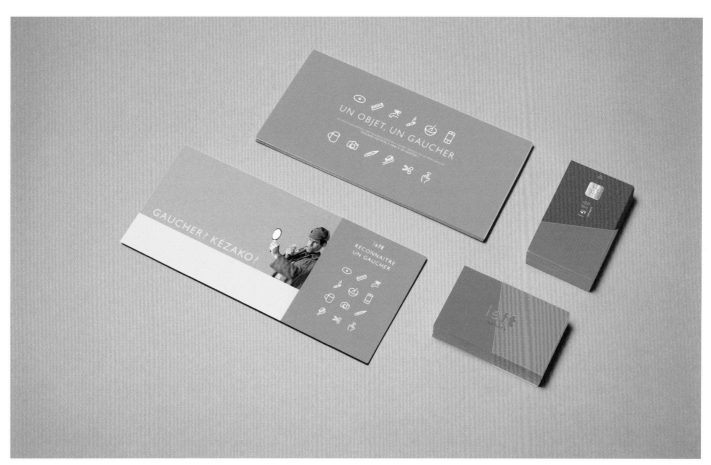

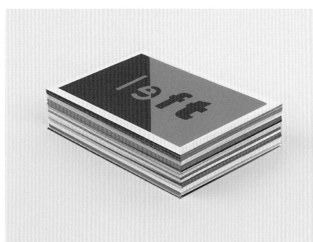

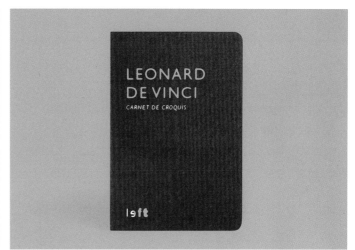

LEFT

LEFT is a concept store that offers cultural products related to left-handed people in order to give a different point of view about them. LEFT gets people interested in left-handed people through their interests: literature, theater, art, music, objects, etc. It is also the opportunity for left-handed people to get objects that suit them.

Design: Arthur Foliard

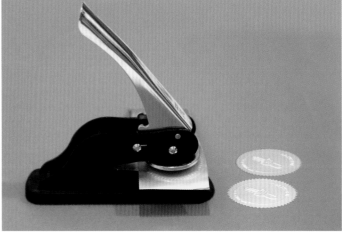

The Ballsies 2014

The Ballsies is the annual awards program for the agency, RE. Judged by some of Australia's leading creative directors, it rewards people for demonstrating 'ballsy' behavior both in work and culture. This year's identity centered on the idea: What's ballsier than telling the truth?

There's nothing quite like awards nights for being all sizzle and no sausage. While they're a great opportunity to celebrate achievement, they're also just a little self-involved. So along with an awareness campaign and merchandise, the Official Guide to the Ballsies took the brave stance of holding a mirror up to awards nights and revealing some of the deeper realities.

Design Agency: RE / Creative Direction: Jason Little
Art Direction & Design: Mick Boston, Olivia King, Shannon Bell
Copywriter: Jason Little, Shannon Bell

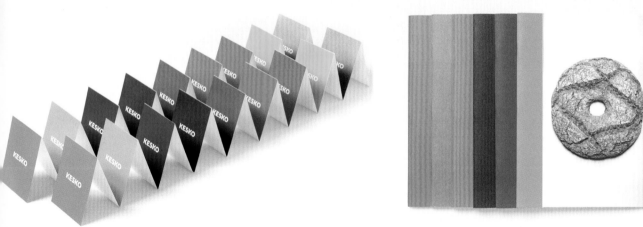

Kesko

Kesko is a leading provider of retail services. Design agency Bond updated their visual identity in a colorful and upbeat way, with a focus on simplicity and timelessness. The highly recognizable corporate logo was also modernized with a delicate touch. The fresh new identity reflected the corporation's entrepreneurial culture and its versatile brand and service portfolio.

Design: Bond Creative Agency

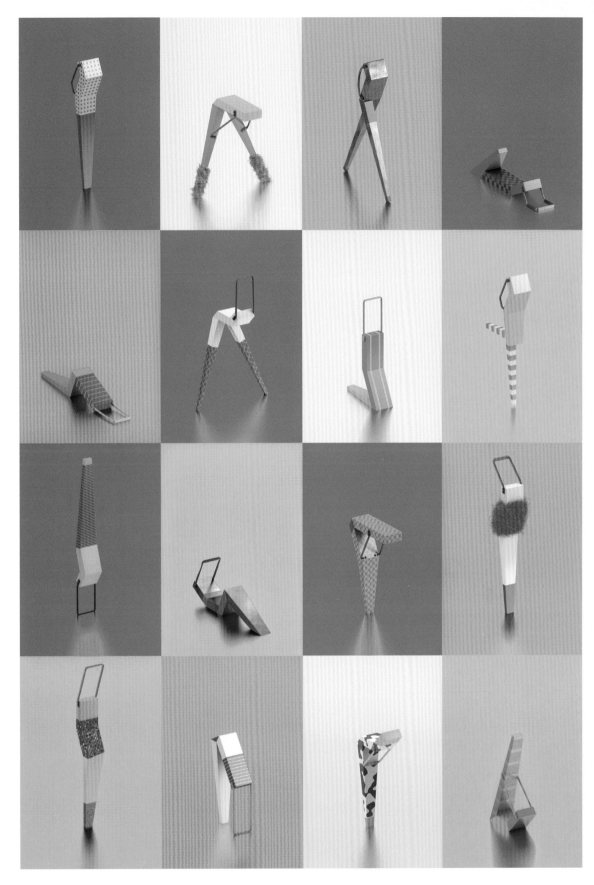

Spring Summer 2012

Giclee print series representing minimalist elegant female silhouettes in seductive stretches and positions.

Design: Fabrice Le Nezet / Photography: Fabrice Le Nezet

151

Not Myself Today

The final event in the month-long Not Myself Today campaign to improve mental health in Canada needed a high-impact installation to engage people and encourage pledges. A wall constructed out of mood pins strategically located in a heavily travelled intersection in the heart of Toronto. The bold rainbow of colors acted as a lightning rod, drawing people in, while the simple act of selecting their mood sparked dialogue, released stories and inspired hundreds of pledges of support.

Design Agency: Blok Design
Creative Direction: Vanessa Eckstein, Marta Cutler
Design: Vanessa Eckstein, Patricia Kleeberg
Copywriter: Marta Cutler

154

STUCK HURT EDGY CRAPPY

SCARED GRUMPY

EVER
HAVE DAYS
WHEN
YOU DON'T
FEEL LIKE
YOURSELF?

NOT myself TODAY

NOTMYSELFTODAY.CA

21°
festival
international
de l'afiche
et du graphisme
de chaumont
29 mai – 20 juin
21st
international
poster and
graphic design
festival
of chaumont
may 29 – june 20

En 2010, le festival s'amuse au jeu
des questions-réponses : "Le graphisme,
qu'est-ce que c'est ??" Question posée
aux étudiants, aux professionnels et au
public dans le cadre des concours et des
expositions, question à laquelle aura à se
confronter le futur Centre International
du Graphisme. Pour y répondre, le festival
se structure cette année en dédiant un
lieu à chaque typologie d'objet graphique :
le logo et l'image animée à la Chapelle,
l'affiche ancienne aux Silos et au Château
du Grand Jardin, l'affiche contemporaine
aux Subsistances, l'illustration dans les
espaces publics, l'expérience au Garage,
la parole au Tri Postal, les jeunes créateurs
dans l'entreprise Tisza Textil. Et c'est
toute la ville qui revêt pour l'occasion
ses habits de fête dessinés par Helmo.
Bonne visite.
    For 2010, the festival asks the same
question to the students, the designers
and the audience: "Graphic design,
qu'est-ce que c'est??". It is the same
question that will ask to itself the future
International Center of Graphic design.
To answer, the festival will be organized
with a specific place for every kind of
graphic stuff: logos and animation in the
Chapelle, historical posters in the Silos
and the Grand Jardin Castle, contemporary
posters in Subsistances, illustration in
public spaces, experimentation in the
Garage, talks in Tri Postal and young
creators in the Tisza Textil factory. By the
way, the town itself will wear its festive
clothes designed by Helmo. Bonne visite.

Etienne Hervy

21st International Poster and Graphic Design Festival of Chaumont

Committed to promoting graphic design for more than 20 years, the city of Chaumont today boasts a valuable collection of historic and contemporary posters. The poster and graphic design festival held in Chaumont every year is one of the major dates in the European graphic design calendar, with exhibitions and competitions recognized throughout the world. For the festival, design studio Helmo created an identity system which helped the city to don its festive garb with colorful strings.

Design: Helmo

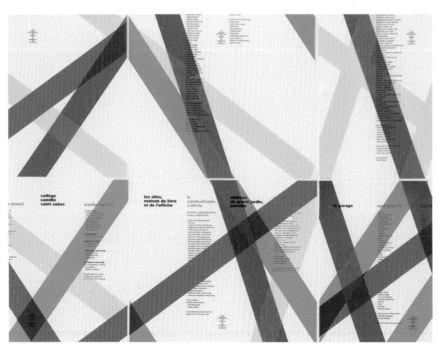

ArtFad 2012

Graphic Identity for ArtFad: Contemporary Art and Craft Awards. The tapes convey parallel paths between art and craft. Design studio Hey made 500 handicraft invitations and the only machinery process was the text printing. As a result, each invitation turned out in a different color and people obtained unique and non-serial pieces.

Design: Hey
Photography: Roc Canals

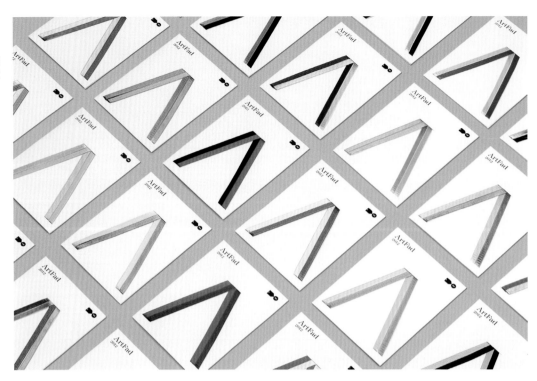

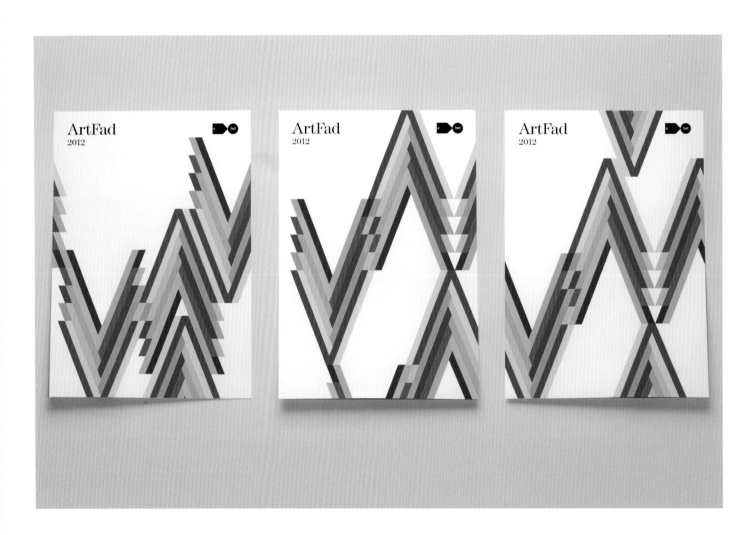

Village Rebranding

Communications and PR agency Village came to design studio colville-walker looking for a new identity to help broaden their reach of clients. Aiming to realign their market position and offering, colville-walker redefined Village's visual language (subsequently shortening the brand from Village Press), stepping away from the black and white go-to fashion aesthetic and introducing a lighter, more design-related look and feel.

Design: colville-walker

QT Port Douglas

QT Port Douglas is the second hotel from the QT
Hotels and Resorts group to open its doors. The QT
Port Douglas/Estilio brand and language eschews the
convention of an identity by capturing the spirit of
place in a visually compelling way – one that portrays
a tropical paradise through distinct personalities
and avoids clichés derived by "tourist" destinations.
Collaboration with Jean-Phillippe Delhomme
presented a new perspective and sets Estilio as an
iconic destination beyond the resort itself. Reflecting
the craft and nuances in the illustration, the identity,
and it's applications are considered in every way, and
delicately crafted with finesse. Overall, the hallmarks
of distinction and quality commensurate with an offer
and destination that is unique.

Design Agency: Fabio Ongarato Design
Creative Direction: Fabio Ongarato
Design: Meg Philips
Illustration: Jean-Phillippe Delhomme

160

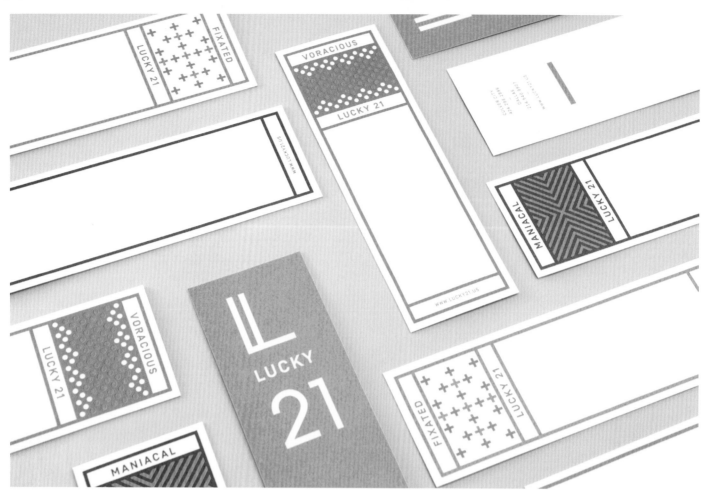

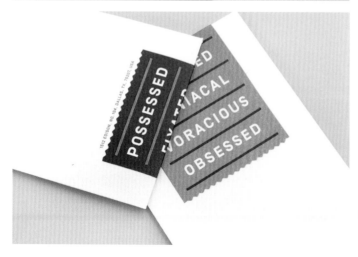

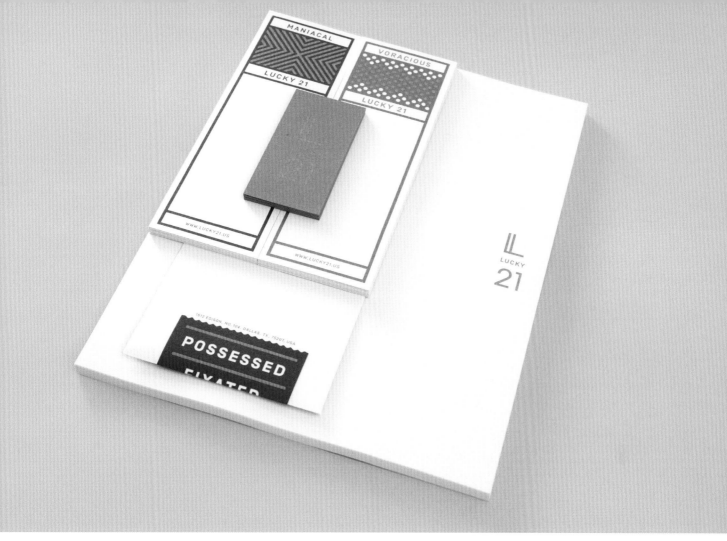

Lucky 21

A film production company in Dallas was ready to take on the highly competitive LA market. They wanted to herald the move with a new identity. A strategic mining session revealed a wonderfully spirited brand character – fiercely passionate and full of humor. The identity balances this off-kilter intensity with a contemporary boldness while allowing the brand's playful voice to shine.

Design Agency: Blok Design / Creative Direction: Vanessa Eckstein, Marta Cutler
Design: Vanessa Eckstein, Emily Tu, Kevin Boothe / Copywriter: Marta Cutler

Sofia by Pelli Clarke Pelli Architects

Sofia is a building designed by architect Cesar Pelli for One Development Group. Located in San Pedro, Mexico, this building not only was designed by an internationally renowned architect, it also has the most generous specifications in every aspect: from automated appliances, to Leed certifications. The task was to communicate such sophistication and exclusiveness to their potential buyers. Opposite of what people usually see for this kind of project, Sofia's identity is formed by three very important axes: logotype, typography and layout.

Design: Anagrama
Photography: Caroga Photographer

Maria Salinas

María Salinas is a Mexican jewelry design shop that creates custom and personalized pieces using gold, silver, precious and semi-precious stones. Maria Salinas wanted a brand that would express the quality and uniqueness of each of their custom pieces, as well as their fine attention to detail.

The brand uses color and typographic subtraction to convey elegance and classic timelessness. Black and gold create the ideal ambiance to bring out the glitz in the brand's jewelry. The logo, with its sublime refinement and simplicity, is reminiscent of those found in high-end fashion brands. Since Maria Salinas offers personalized pieces where, together with the client she exchanges and sketches ideas, tangible grid patterns were integrated throughout the branding and the shop's interior design.

Design: Anagrama
Photography: Caroga Photographer

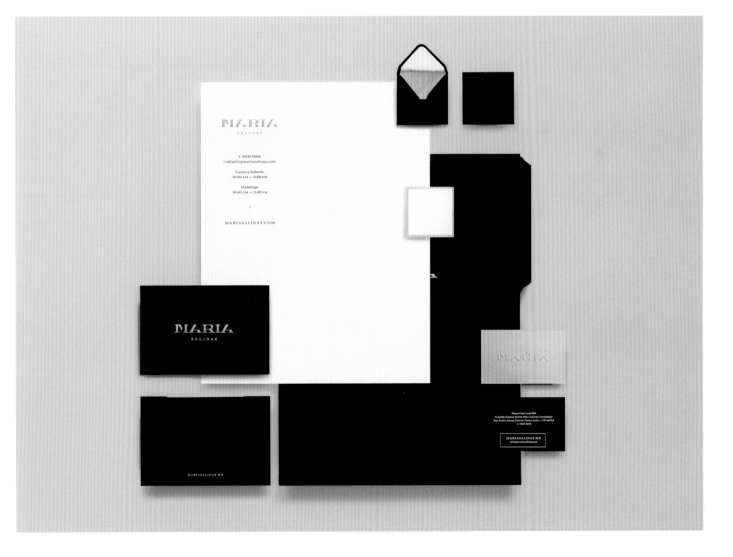

Optica Cid Concept Store Branding

The aim of the project was to find and achieve a shopping experience for the customer away from the current settings of these kinds of spaces. The clinical character blends with the aspect of fashion eyewear, creating a clean visual and an elegant boutique language, in which the fashion gives an added value to the product, gets the loyalty of customer, and transforms a buyer into a potential follower of the brand.

Design: MABAA™ / Copywriter: MABAA™ / Photography: MABAA™, Hector Santos-Diez

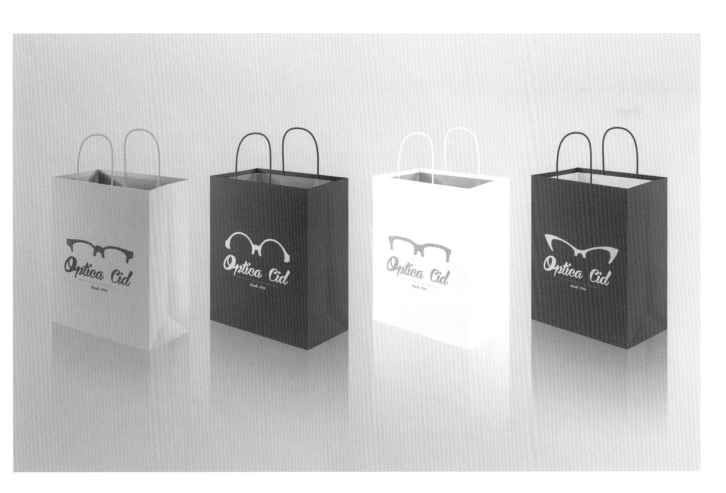

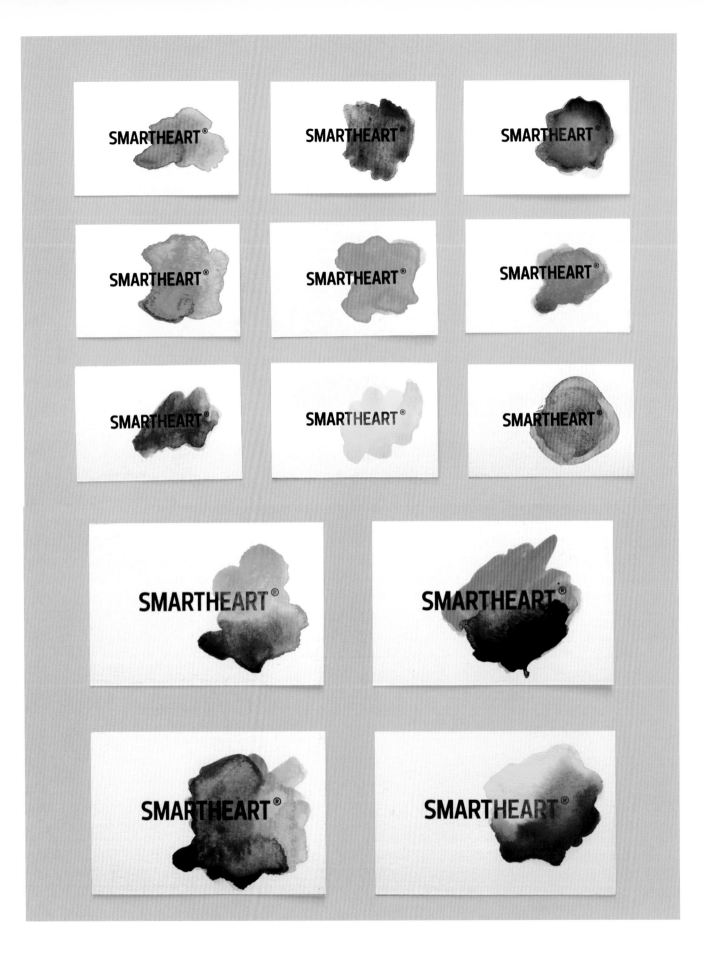

Emotionalisation of SmartHeart

A variation of identity for SmartHeart Agency. A series of business cards with increased emotional component.

Design Agency: SmartHeart / Design: Yuriy Mihalchenko

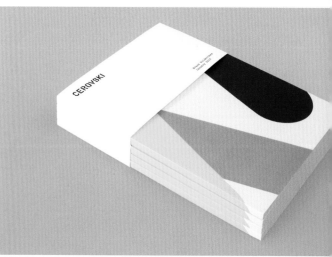

Cerovski

Cerovski is a young Croatian print production studio that revels in the challenge of "nebulous finishing, microscopic editions, absurd materials and crazy deadlines." Design agency Bunch developed a new brand identity for the studio – which included a custom logotype and typeface, website, and a variety of printed collateral – that delivers a distinctive contrast of utility and creative flourish, technology and individualized service, through stencil cut type, a number of material choices and print finishes, and a personalized but digitally generated daily planner.

Design Agency: Bunch / Creative Direction: Denis Kovac

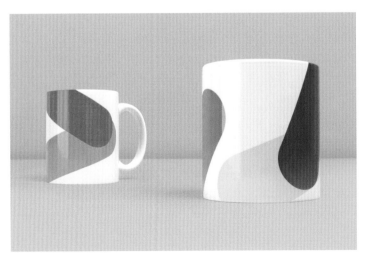

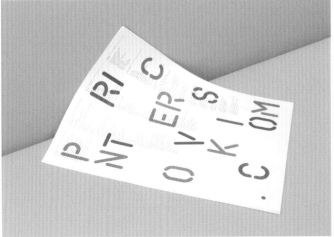

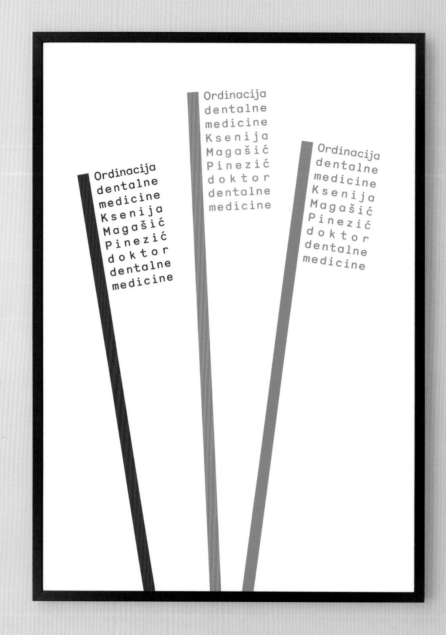

KMP KMP KMP

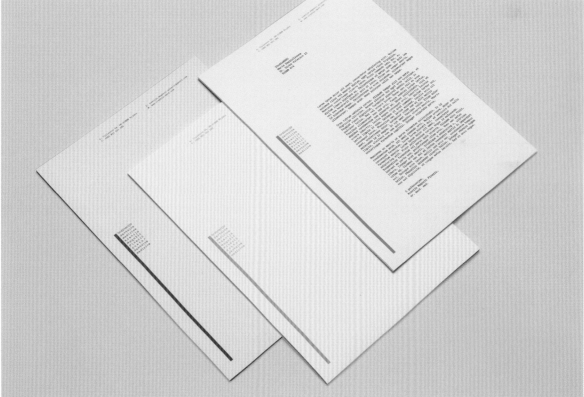

Dr. Magasic Pinezic

An identity, stationery, responsive website and signage for a dental practice based in Rijeka, Croatia. In order to take advantage of the rather long name of the practice, the logotype is constructed from a thick vertical line and fully justified typography arranged in a way to get an abstracted toothbrush – a reminder of the importance of a good dental hygiene.

Design Agency: Studio8585 / Design: Mario Depicolzuane

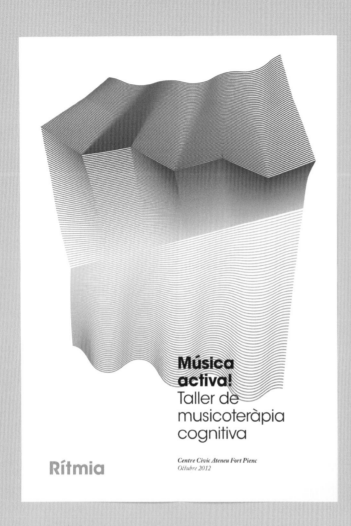

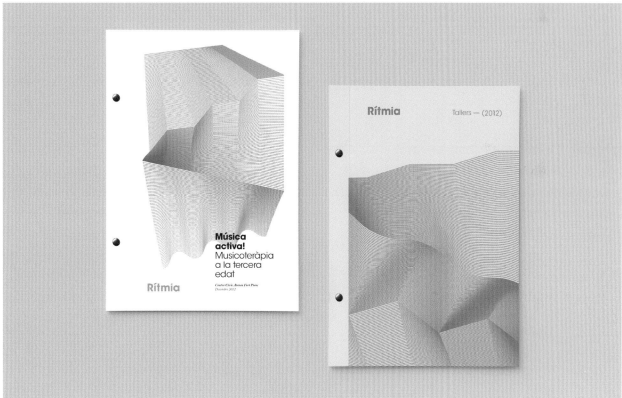

Rítmia

Identity for the social music therapist and educator Celia Castillo. The identity was based on graphic representations of the rhythmic exercises that Celia used to treat her patients. The basic aim was to provoke different moods in them.

Design Agency: Atipus / Design: Albert Estruch

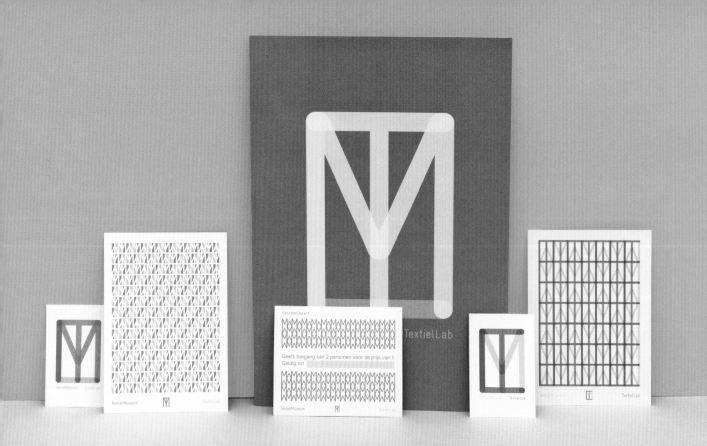

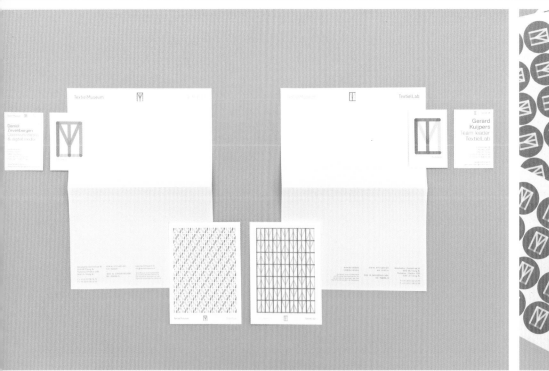

TextielMuseum & TextielLab

The unique character of the TextielMuseum is the combination with its development facility – the TextielLab. Next to hosting exhibitions about textile and design, the Lab develops textile projects with contemporary designers. In the identity the focus is on visualizing the combination of these two characters of the institution. The basic icon of the institute represents the T, M and L that are overlapping. By multiplying the letters different opacities and color combinations are created. In the icon the weight can shift as well to either TM or TL representing TextielMuseum or TextielLab. Departing from the icon it serves as the basic element to construct a big variety of patterns. The dynamic character of this system allows to implement the pattern on several parts of the identity like stationary, packaging, website etc. Making a visual link to textile patterns it permanently communicates the logo and iconography of the Museum and Lab in a subtle way.

Design: Raw Color
Photography: Raw Color

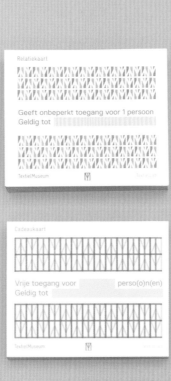

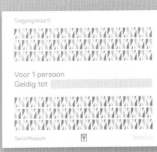

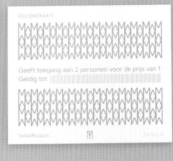

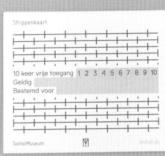

177

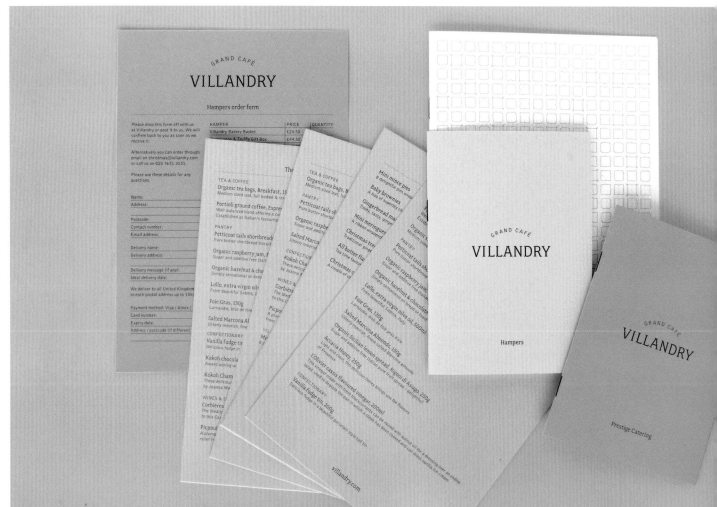

Villandry

Villandry is an all-day French restaurant, cafe, foodstore, bakery and bar located in London and Bicester Village. Mind Design developed the identity, packaging, signage system and all printed materials. The identity was based on a set of five shapes which refer to traditional brasserie menu frames. The shapes were either used individually or combined to create a pattern. A bright color scheme was chosen in contrast to the classic shapes.

Design: Mind Design

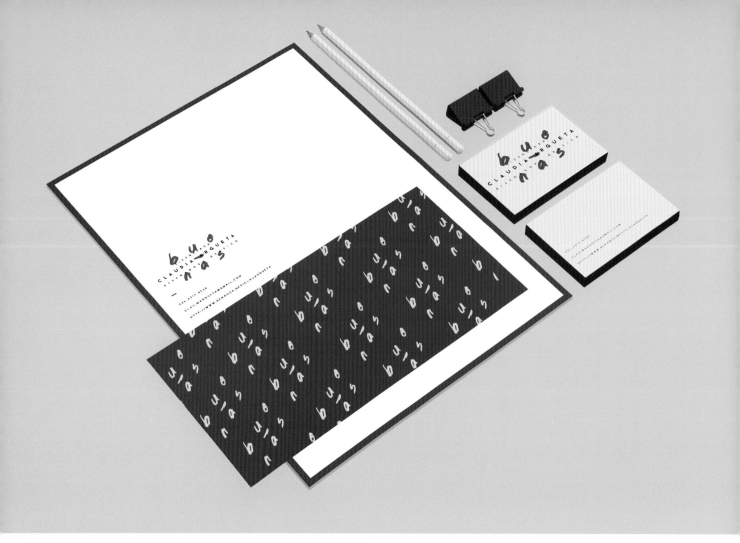

Buenas

This project was Claudia Argueta's self branding. Her identity was captured by the correct selection of the color palette, typeface and manners of speech showcasing her work aesthetics. "Buenas" is a colloquial expression in Guatemala, used commonly as a greeting. And it can be translated as "Hey there!"

Design: Claudia Argueta Aragón

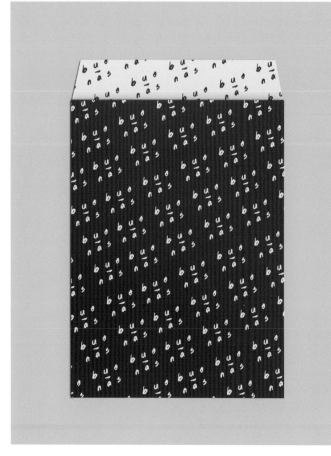

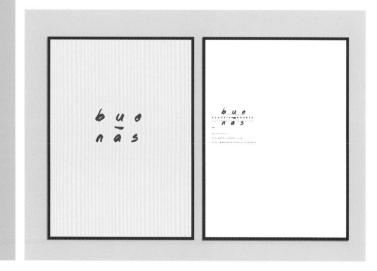

Via XX Settembre

Identity design for a family run business from the harbor town of Genova who makes and distributes organic food items. A patterned textile with a distinct color scheme inspired from the sea was consistently used on all packaging, making it stand out, and easy to recognize. The labels were kept very simple, yet informative, and the typefaces chosen were inspired by Italian culture. The crest used in the logo and on the packaging emphasized the family aspect.

Design: Marius Wathne

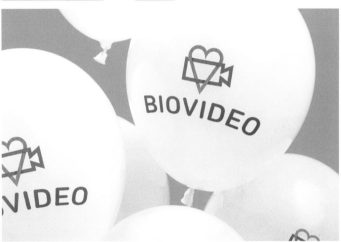

Biovideo

Biovideo is a company heartfully built with the purpose of helping new parents live and enjoy the amazing experience of their baby's first moments. Capturing the baby's first days at the hospital, the movie is uploaded online ready to view and share with the world. The company believes that every baby should have his or her very own Biovideo so, thanks to alliances with partners such as Johnson's Baby and New York Life, they provide this service for free at select partner hospitals around the Unites States and Mexico. The branding proposal uses rounded type and a carefully chosen color palette to communicate the brand's heartfelt friendliness. It is simple, clear and inspires warmth and trust. The icon ties emotion with technology, a symbol of Biovideo's extraordinary storytelling venture. The predominantly white and baby blue color palette transmits baby vibes while the striking but limited use of red is enough to prevent it from falling into unremarkable cliché.

Design: Anagrama / Photography: Caroga Photographer

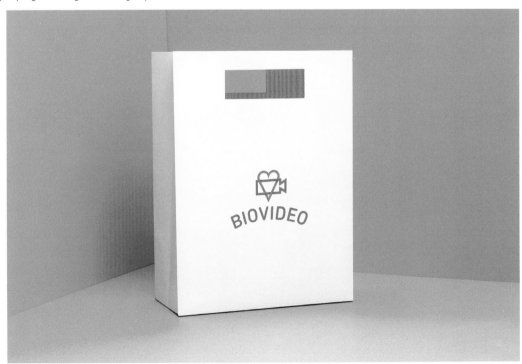

Crack.

Crack. is a creative agency
handling branding, web design, and
packaging. The brief was to create
the direct mailer for clients. The box
contains a brochure, a name-card,
a packet of cookies and tea, with
the concept: "Let us do the thinking,
enjoy your tea time."

Design: Audy Irwantoro, Christopher
Pambudi, Keshia Anindita

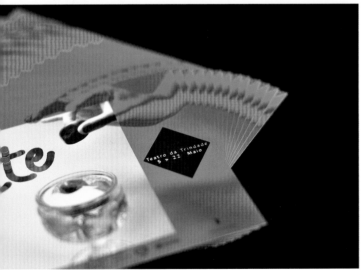

Á Espera de Gorete

Á Espera de Gorete is a theatre play about the actual social situation in Portugal, composed by a series of absurd and hilarious sketches, with the purpose of instilling a very serious sense of vindication.
To fit this aesthetics of the absurd, the graphics were designed as colorful and ostentatious as the theatre play. The promotional materials included several poster formats, and a postcard distributed everywhere in the city of Lisbon.

Design: Paulo Lopes / Copywriter: Mafalda Santos / Photography: Paulo Lopes

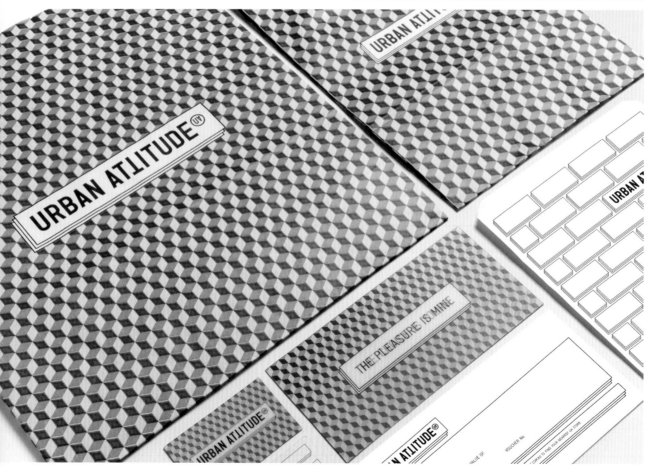

Urban Attitude

Urban Attitude is a novelty gift store with a long-standing cult following in Melbourne.
With new owners and an intention for retail expansion nationally, Fabio Ongarato Design was commissioned to undertake an extensive review process, a business brand strategy that culminated in the redevelopment of the 'total brand experience.'
With a renewed focus, the identity manifests in a vernacular of 'custom labels' and 'optical patterns' applied to lenticular lenses giving it further dynamic dimension. The rebrand encompassed everything from collateral to packaging, realizing a new store model which encompassed merchandising, streetscape flags and illuminated signage.

Design: Fabio Ongarato Design / Photography: Sharyn Cairns

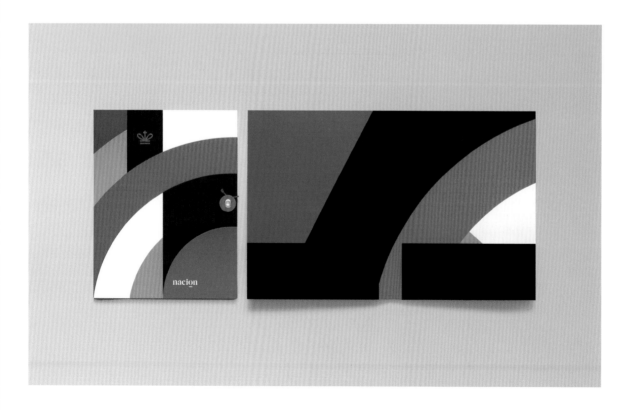

Nacion

Nacion is a multi-purpose real-estate development project located in Monterrey, Mexico. With space for apartment homes, offices and stores, Nacion aims to be the ultimate all-in-one community for its residents. This branding proposal takes that feeling of community and elevates it, creating a tactile sense of belonging, a nationalist pride. Design agency Anagrama took visual elements and symbols from flags and official governmental papers, such as passports and seals, and simplified and remixed them with bright, fun colors to create a modern look. With this project, Anagrama designed with the mentality of creating the identity of a brand new country.

Design: Anagrama
Photography: Caroga Photographer

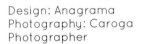

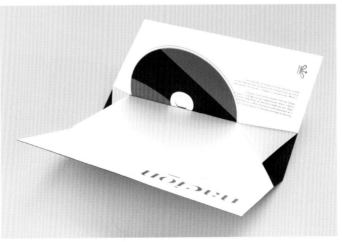

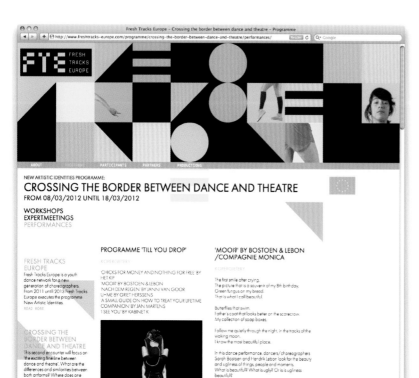

190

Fresh Tracks Europe

Fresh Tracks Europe is a youth dance network for a new generation of choreographers. Their new identity was based on a set of dancing body parts and colored shapes. With these building blocks design agency Trapped in Suburbia created an identity with lots of room to play. It symbolized the philosophy of Fresh Tracks Europe, where the different European dance groups work together to create a new dance generation. There were two directions in the identity. For internal communication the white version was used, while for the external communication the black version was used. The identity consisted of logo, colors, animations, stationary, business cards, posters, flyers, banners, leaflets and the website.

Client: Het Lab / Design Agency: Trapped in Suburbia / Creative Direction: Cuby Gerards, Karin Langeveld
Art Direction: Cuby Gerards, Karin Langeveld / Design: Cuby Gerards, Karin Langeveld, Sebastian Pataki

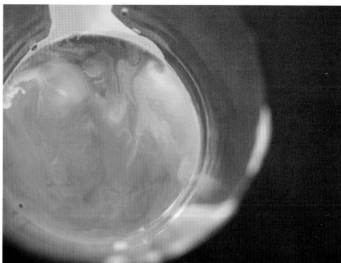

IS Creative Studio Cards

IS Creative Studio is a Madrid-based design consultancy, operating in a global marketplace. Founded in 2010, the concept and goal of IS Creative Studio is to be an important platform for creativity and design with simplicity as the operating philosophy. Designer Richars Meza created a bold and minimalistic logotype to capture the simplicity philosophy in their graphic identity. Original and attractive, the business cards were designed not only as a communication piece, but as a design object.

Design Agency: IS Creative Studio / Design: Richars Meza

Salon Nemetz

Some things can't be described – they have to be experienced. Christina Nemetz is one of them. And she's also a hairdresser who is passionate about her work, offering outstanding advice and immensely skilled services. The corporate design expressed the versatility and adaptability of Christina Nemetz. The business cards were designed in eight different layouts in two colors, printed on 30 different materials – totaling 480 opportunities for individual expression.

Design: Designliga

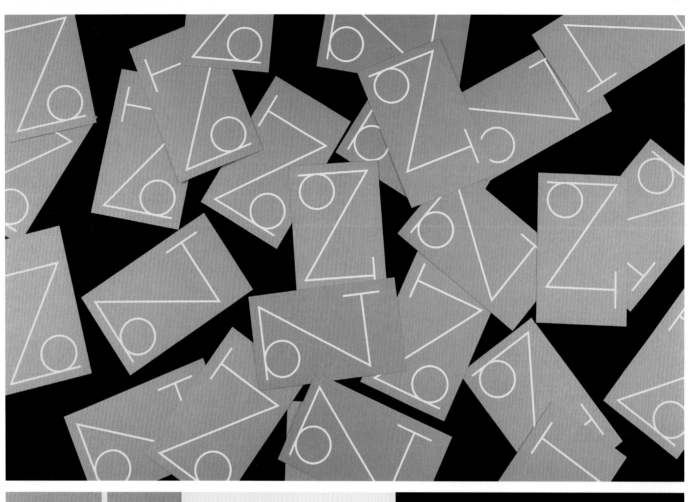

BNT Studio

Corporate identity for BNT Studio, a distribution studio specializing in industrial design and innovation products. BNT is the exclusive distributor of the Jake Dyson brand in Canada. BNT's identity was developed to reflect characteristics that are common to the products and brands they distribute. Working closely with BNT, designer Emanuel Cohen aimed to design a minimalistic, futuristic and streamlined mark with a distinct personality.

Design Agency: 26 Lettres / Design: Emanuel Cohen

Helsinki Food Company

Helsinki Food Company provides design and production services to food industry and other industries close by. Basically, they do everything that involves food consulting or food styling: from developing recipes to producing TV-shows and media productions. Design agency Werklig was commissioned to design a versatile, easily modified and cost-efficient brand identity stemming from the celebration of food culture.

Design: Werklig

198

Massproductions

Design agency BrittonBritton was responsible for Massproductions' visual identity and communication design. Mixing with a structural, typographical authority with craft textures and confidently appropriating an upholstered color palette of the past, they created a simple and clean graphic identity for this Swedish interior design company to break through the global market.

Design: BrittonBritton

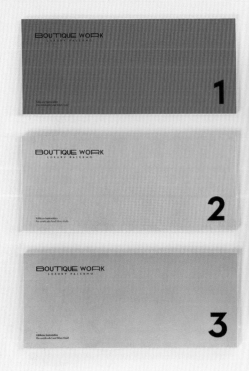

Boutique Work

Boutique Work celebrates the intersection between sustainable architecture, innovative design, luxury and Palermo's identity and essence. An office complex development that comprises three boutique office buildings with different identities but a unique urban language.
Design studio Estudio FBDI was in charge of creating the full brand identity including naming the project. The studio initially focused on creating a strong concept for the brand and started by defining the most symbolic and differentiating aspects of the project. They then designed its visual identity, graphic language and applications creating a system that represents the projects spirit and uniqueness. Contrasts, juxtapositions and musical rhythms are some of the aspects defined as essentials to the overall look and feel of the brand, and with that idea as a starting point they created a visual identity that portrays a luxury code mixed with Palermo's vibrant spirit.

Design: Estudio FBDI
Photography: Estudio FBDI

1 2 3
BOUTIQUE WORK
LUXURY PALERMO

BOUTIQUEWORKLUXURYPALERMOBOUTIQUEWORKLUXURYPALERMOBOUTIQUEWORKLUXURYPALERMOBOUTIQUEWORKLUXURYPALERMOBOUTIQUEWORKLUXURYPALERMOBOUTIQUEWORKLUXURYPALERMOBOUTIQUEWORKLUXURYPALERMOBOUTIQUEWORKLUXURYPALERMOBOUTIQUEWORKLUXURYPALERMOBOUTIQUEWORKLUXURYPALERMOBOUTIQUEWORKLUXURYPALERMOBOUTIQUEWORKLUXURYPALERMOBOUTIQUEWORKLUXURYPALERMOBOUTIQUEWORKLUXURYPALERMOBOUTIQUEWORKLUXURYPALERMO

BOUT
IQUE
WORK
LUXU
RYPA
LERMO

CIN | Goethe Institute

The Cultural Innovators Networks (CIN) is a joint project of more than 20 Goethe-Institutes around the Mediterranean, coordinated by the Goethe-Institut Alexandria. It is a platform for communication, exchange and learning provided for young active civil society members from Europe and the MENA region.

CIN is seizing this momentum to bring together creative thinkers from around the Mediterranean and Germany. Through an exchange of ideas and experiences, participants will take home new ideas and impact their societies through positive, cultural change.

Designer Salma Shamel was commissioned to create a visual identity for the network and its collaterals including brochures, flyers, banners and stationary that were distributed in events held in countries such as Egypt, Tunisia, Turkey, Italy and Germany.

Design: Salma Shamel / Photography: Claudia Wiens

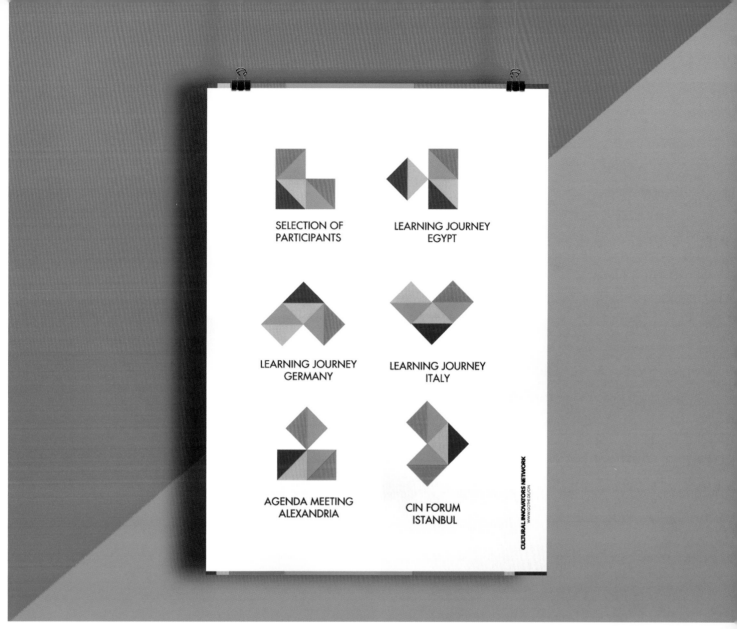

SELECTION OF
PARTICIPANTS

LEARNING JOURNEY
EGYPT

LEARNING JOURNEY
GERMANY

LEARNING JOURNEY
ITALY

AGENDA MEETING
ALEXANDRIA

CIN FORUM
ISTANBUL

CULTURAL INNOVATORS NETWORK
WWW.GOETHE.DE/CIN

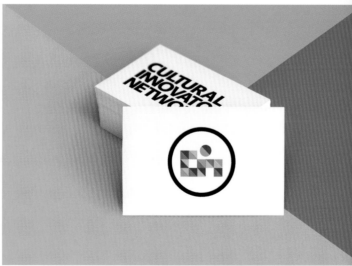

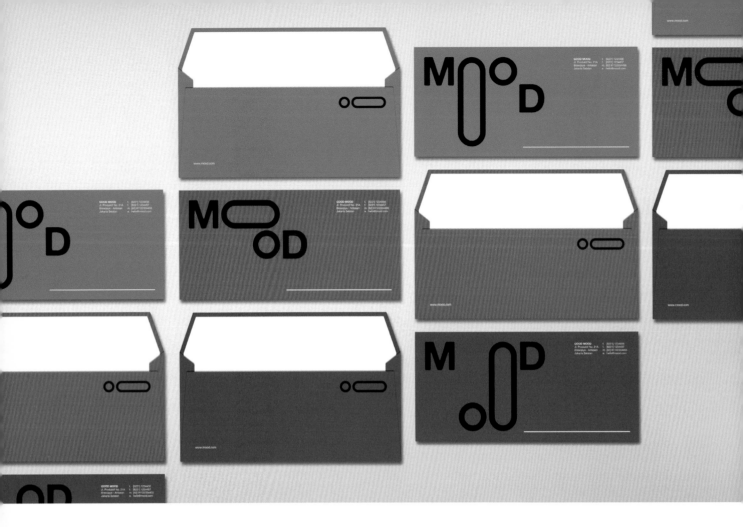

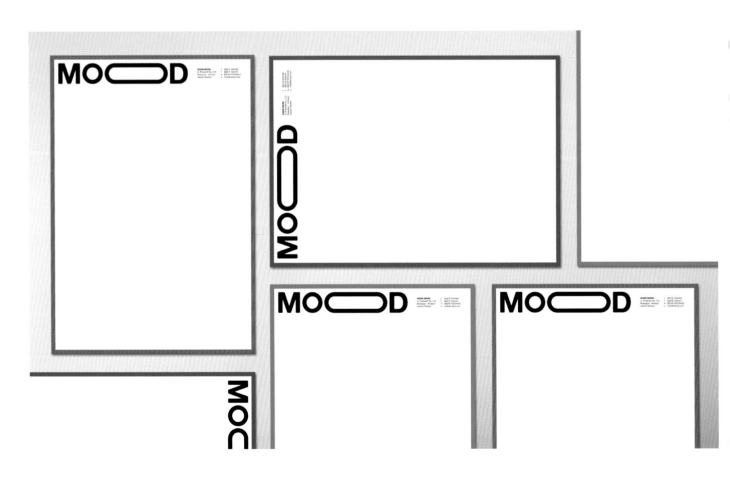

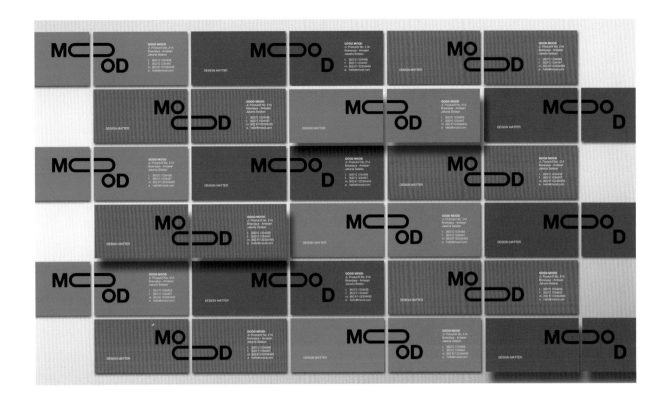

Mood

This was a personal project created by designer Zaky Arifin. Arifin tried to explore how a 'noun' becomes an expressive logo, simply playing with typography and using digital RGB basic colors (red, green and blue as the expression of angry, happy and sad).

Design Agency: Studio Minor
Designe: Zaky Arifin

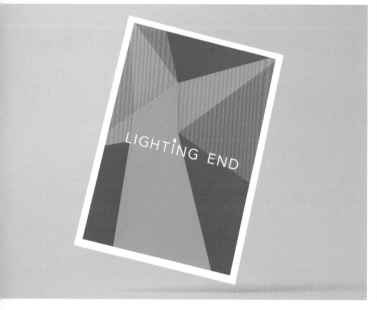

Lighting End

Lighting End is an industrial design agency specializing in lamp design. Designer Andrea Ramirez and María José Torrero developed the whole branding idea around the power of light coming out of fire. The colors reflected the young spirit of the company and their modern vision towards design.

Creative Direction: Andrea Ramirez
Art Direction: María José Torrero
Design: María José Torrero
Illustration: Andrea Ramirez
Photography: Andrea Ramirez

Doctor Manzana

Design Agency Masquespacio's project for Doctor Manzana, a store specializing in technical services for smartphones and tablets, besides being a seller of design gadgets for mobile devices. The project included the redesign of Doctor Manzana's branding and the realization of the design for their first point of sale located in Valencia, Spain. Ana Milena Hernández Palacios, creative director of Masquespacio said: "Talking about the colors as we started from a company name allied with a doctor we wanted to create a concept based on a hospital, however as we didn't want to create a conventional design, we discarded this option, but maintaining blue and green colors as a reference to the first word in the company's brand name." Looking at the store everything starts from the striking facade that incorporates the same angles and colors like for the graphic identity. The blue and green colors like a reference to the doctor, the salmon color for the fashionistas and the purple for the freaks.

Design Agency: Masquespacio
Design: Ana Milena Hernández Palacios
Photography: David Rodríguez

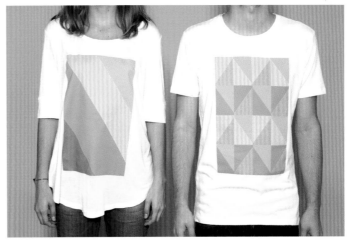

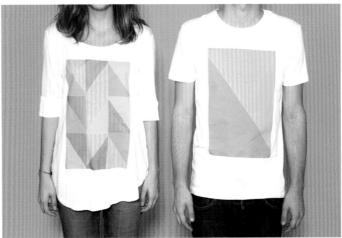

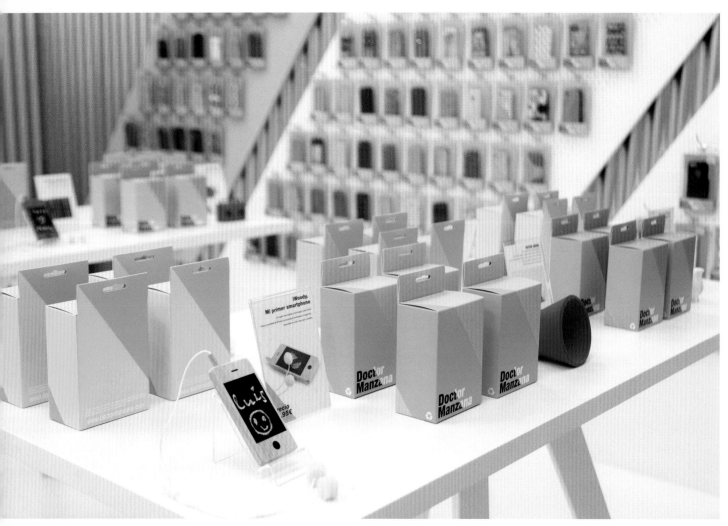

Léa Munsch

Léa Munsch provides the clients with creative management, so that they can focus on the core creative part of their work and have the management of the business side of the activity. Design studio Hey was responsible for the personal identity of Léa Munsch. Three different colors – green, purple and orange – created an innovative and harmonious atmosphere. Simple design reflected the efficiency, functionality and spirit of the brand.

Design: Hey / Photography: Roc Canals

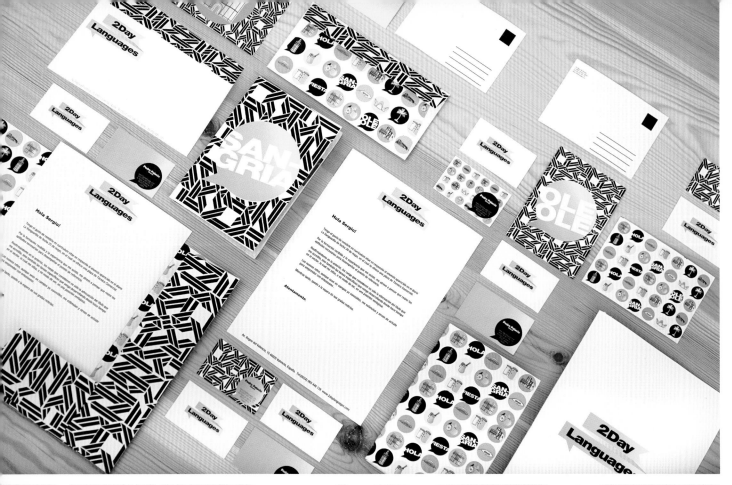

2Day Languages

Design studio Masquespacio was commissioned to design a Spanish school for young foreign students from between 20 and 30 years old. Fresh and actual pastel colors together with a mix of wooden furniture were used to attract attention from young kids. A fresh and actual identity ideal to attract cool young kids.

Design Agency: Masquespacio
Design: Ana Milena Hernández Palacios
Photography: David Rodríguez

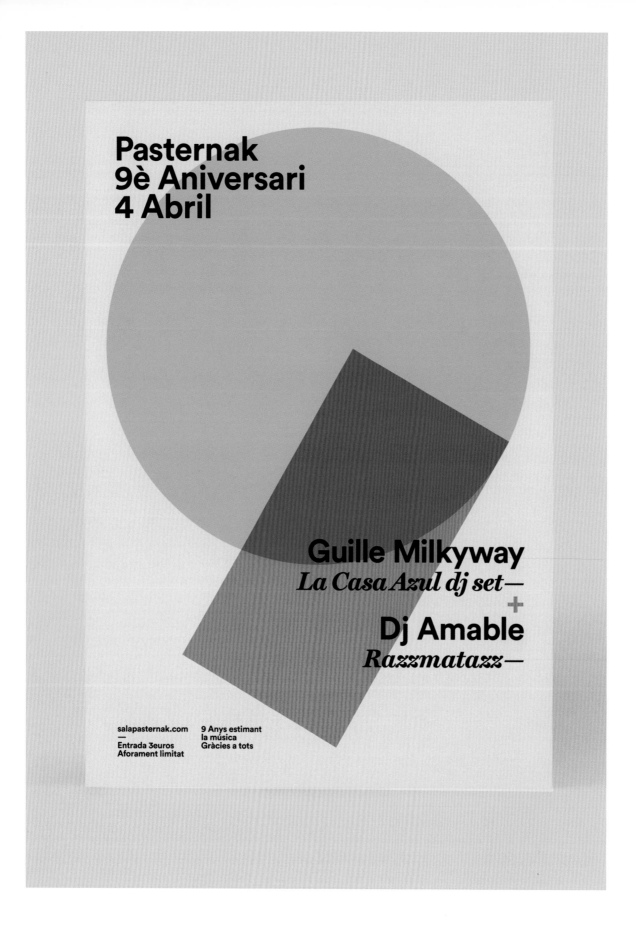

216

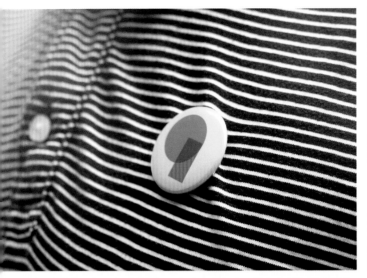

Poster text:

Pasternak
9è Aniversari
4 Abril

Guille Milkyway
La Casa Azul dj set—
+
Dj Amable
Razzmatazz—

salapasternak.com
Entrada 3euros
Aforament limitat

9 Anys estimant
la música
Gràcies a tots

9th Anniversary of Sala Pasternak

Print design by designer Quim Marin for Sala Pasternak's annual campaign. With a sense of modernism, this identity is based on type, color blocking and geometry. The number 9 includes a circle and a square.

Design: Quim Marin

218

Flowergala

Over the past 35 years, Polytrade Paper Corporation has been introducing different overseas paper brands, and innovative paper uses to markets and users. This time, Polytrade brought people Astrobrights papers, which comes in 23 bright colors and attracts people's attention. To launch this new paper series, Polytrade held a launch party in a restaurant in Macau, China. Design agency BLOW was asked to create the event name, identity, promotional materials, and decoration for the event.

Design Agency: BLOW
Design: Ken Lo, Crystal Cheung, Caspar Ip
Copywriter: Ken Lo

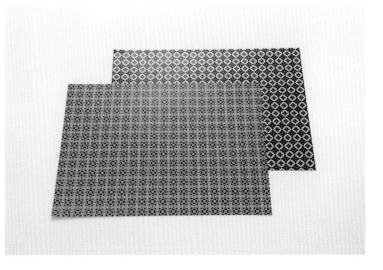

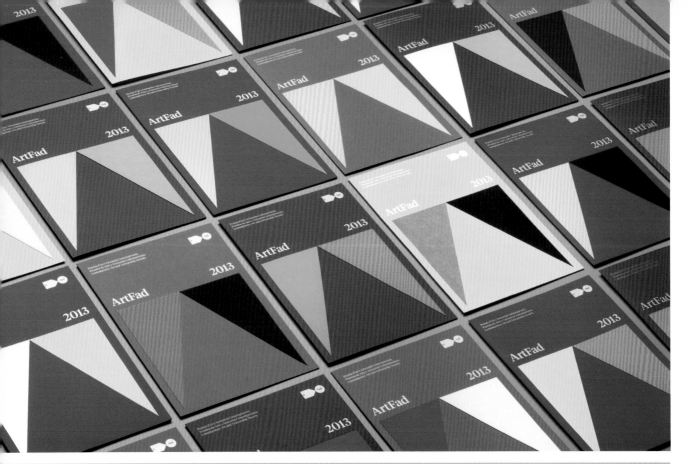

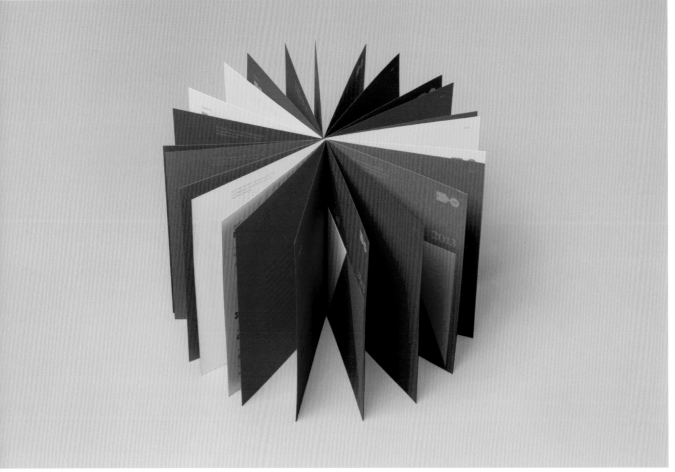

ArtFad 2013

Artfad is a ceremony held each year in Barcelona rewarding contemporary art and craft. Design studio Hey created the graphic identity of this event for the 2013 edition. They produced 500 handcrafted invitations by sticking colored triangles one by one to create the letter "A". The only machinery process was the text printing. As a result, each invitation turned out in a different color and people obtained unique and non-serial pieces.

Design: Hey / Photography: Roc Canals

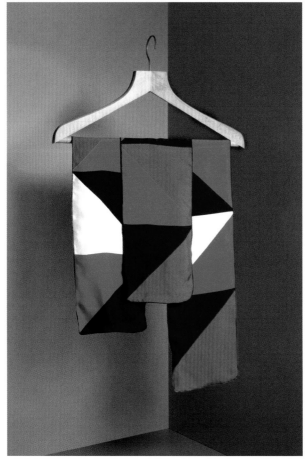

Scotland and Venice

Curated by the Common Guild for the 55th Venice Biennale, the exhibition introduced three artists within the historic 15th century Palazzo Pisani. The identity articulates the trio through overlapping colors, projecting a confident and distinct identity that stands out in the multi-layered complexity of La Biennale. The exhibition tables were made by Derek Welsh Studio.

Design: Graphical House
Photography: Graphical House

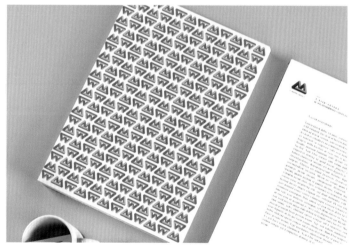

My identity.

The Penrose triangle is an impossible object. It was originally created by Oscar Reutersvärd, rediscovered by Roger Penrose and now reused by graphic designer Maria Jose. Jose modified the form to look like an M for Maria (the designer's name). "I always liked the idea of doing something impossible. That's why I chose the Penrose triangle as the root of my personal logo design," said the designer.

Design: María José Torrero Heredia / Copywriter: María José Torrero Heredia
Photography: María José Torrero Heredia

224

Match Idea

Branding proposal for a web design agency called Match Ideas. The main focus was to create a modern and eye-catching identity using bright colors and a simple yet powerful logo. Designer Andrea Ramírez Sabat played with the idea of matches and fire, turning the "i" into a match. For the color palette, she chose purple, the tone previously used for the agency, and added a bright aqua color to make it more playful and young.

Design: Andrea Ramírez Sabat

LUMA (Concept Identity)

As a thesis for the Senior Year at Buenos Aires University, designer Stephanie Helou was asked to make up an imaginary festival. Helou decided to work on the glam universe, conceiving the schedule of the festival as a system itself. With music in its centre and satellite activities –art, photography, theatre, film and fashion–, Luma would integrate different disciplines to amuse everyone who became part of it. Vibrant and eye-caching colors, simple and clean layouts, were the means to achieve a fresh modern look inspired in space, astrology, light and wildness. The event would take place in the Zoo, so wild cats turned out to be the main characters of these pieces.

Design: Stephanie Helou / Copywriter: Stephanie Helou

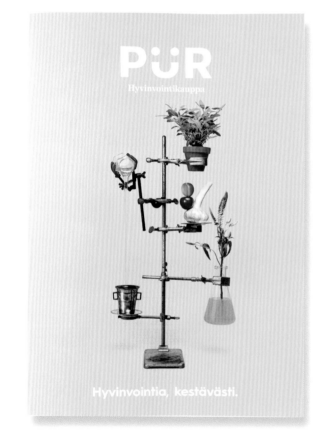

PUR

PUR is a new generation of wellness shops in Helsinki, bringing various aspects of healthy living together under one roof. Design agency Bond created a complete branding concept that covered everything from the brand identity to the shop design, website, photography, advertising and marketing collaterals. All this helps PUR to communicate its message of holistic wellbeing in an appealing, fun and informative way.

Design Agency: Bond Creative Agency
Creative Direction: Arttu Salovaara
Design: Aleksi Hautamäki, Toni Hurme, Janne Norokytö, Annika Peltoniemi, Jesper Bange, Lawrence Dorrington
Photography: Osmo Puuperä

www.rawcolor.nl

RAW COLOR
INDEX
COLLECTION—
TEA TOWELS
'A RESEARCH
ABOUT COLOUR
WITHIN WEAVING.
INDEXING THE
SHADES OF EACH
SURFACE BY THE
USE OF SQUARES
REPRESENTING
10 TILL 100
PERCENT.'

100% Cotton, produced at TextielLab Tilburg, The Netherlands

Index Collection

Indexing color in the technique of weaving was the departure point of this research. The whole project evolved at the TextielLab in Tilburg, a workplace to develop and produce textiles. The Index Collection is series of tea towels and blankets. The total collection consists of 3 different color series. Each series follows the same process, from Monotone, through Duotone, to Multitone, with the first shade taking the lead and a new tone will be added in the following step. The "index" is especially designed to translate the amount of color within each surface, by the usage of squares representing 10% to 100%.

Design: Raw Color / Photography: Raw Color

INDEX

advance society and business alike. Blok's work has received critical recognition around the world and has been exhibited in museums from Tokyo to Toronto.

P026-027, P091, P116-117, P152-155, P162-163

BLOW

www.blow.hk

BLOW is a Hong Kong based design studio founded by a renowned young designer, Ken Lo, in 2010. Specialized in branding, identities, packaging, environmental graphics, print, publications and website design, they provide clients with mind-blowing design with simple and bold approach that helps the brand to stand out from the crowd.

P068-071, P218-219

Bold

www.boldstockholm.se

Bold is a part of the Åkestam Holst group, which includes one of Sweden's largest and best advertising agencies Åkestam Holst as well as the brand experience agency Knock and the retail/CRM agency Promenad and the production agency Studion. They strongly believe in the cross fertilization between their different competences and together they can deliver a full service communication offering.

P036-037

Bond

www.bond.fi

Bond is a versatile creative agency founded by designers with different specialties. Their skill set covers strategic, graphic, product, digital and retail design. Their creative work always starts at the core of a brand, based on which they create a lot of practical ideas for brand behavior. Together with the client, they identify the best ones.

P142-143, P150, P228-229

BrittonBritton

www.brittonbritton.com

BrittonBritton, founded in 1992 by Christina and Claes Britton, is a creative branding and communication agency that helps companies and organizations to launch, develop and clarify their brands and to market their services and products. They work with all available tools and media to achieve optimal results for their clients – strategic analysis, market analysis, graphic design, photography, web, advertising, print, retail communication, film,

contract publishing, exhibitions and events, architecture and other three dimensional configuration, and PR including social media.

P076, 077, P199

Bunch

www.bunchdesign.com

Bunch is a leading creative design studio offering a diverse range of work, including, identity, literature, editorial, digital and motion. Established in 2002 with an international reach, from London to Zagreb, Bunch has an in-house team of specialists to deliver intelligent and innovative cross-platform solutions of communication design. Over the years Bunch has been commissioned by many blue chip companies as well as younger brands and artistic industries. Building an impressive client base that covers many styles and disciplines, such as BBC, Nike, Diesel, Sony, Sky, Red Bull and others.

P126-127, P170-171

BVD

http://bvd.se

BVD is a design and branding agency specialized in strategic design. Together with their clients, they move brands and make them innovative, sustainable and continuously profitable. BVD regards design as a powerful strategic tool and believes that a successful project does not only require exceptional creativity, but also thoughtful analysis, a high level of business orientation and in-depth knowledge of market conditions. Through the years they have delivered a vast number of successful design projects for leading global brands with outstanding, measurable results.

P114-115

C

Claudia Argueta

www.behance.net/clauargueta

Claudia Argueta is a graphic designer from Guatemala. Graduated from Rafael Landivar University with a bachelor's degree in graphic design, Claudia has six years of experience in the field and started out as a freelance graphic designer with a variety of experience in editorial design, poster design, advertising, web, branding and identity design. Claudia has a profound passion for minimalistic projects because of the enormous beauty that can be found in something so very simple. Her main purpose is to aim for

simplicity and objectivity. Reducing works to the fundamental, the essential and the necessary and striping away the ornamental layers, Claudia believes that clean, simple and functional design matters.

P180

Codefrisko

www.codefrisko.be

Codefrisko is a Graphic Design & Art direction studio which was founded in 2006 by Audrey Schayes (founder of Frisko design) and Thomas Wyngaard (co-founder of Code Magazine Belgium). Codefrisko is specialized in Culture, Fashion, Architecture, Design and the Food industry. Their expertise ranges from acting as a think tank to doing global strategy, graphic design, photos shoots, providing online solutions, and much more.

P079

colville-walker

www.colville-walker.com

colville-walker is a London-based multidisciplinary studio specializing in design and art direction for the fashion industry. Founded and led by creative director Chris Colville-Walker, their design team is committed to producing well-crafted design, innovative ideas and unforgettable experiences, working in partnership with fashion, luxury and lifestyle brands to deliver ambitious, engaging and successful results. Through collaboration with artists, photographers and creative talent the studio works across a wide range of projects, from art direction and image development, brand positioning and identity, retail environments and window displays, to event production and set design, graphic and digital design, and rich editorial content.

P159

Cristina Bianchi

www.cristinabianchi.it

Cristina Bianchi, 1985, is an Italian graphic designer and art director based in Vienna, Austria. She studied communication design at the Politecnico University in Milan and at the Universität für Angewandte Kunst in Vienna. She has worked in Italy and Austria for different agencies developing experience in graphic design and art direction, editorial and print design, packaging, branding and visual identity.

P016-017

D

Daigo Daikoku

http://daikoku.ndc.co.jp

Born in Hiroshima Prefecture in 1979, Daigo Daikoku is an art director and graphic designer who joined Nippon Design Center Inc. after graduating from the Visual Communication Design Course at Kanazawa College of Art in 2003. Daikoku worked for Hara Design Institute until establishing Daikoku Design Institute in 2011. Daikoku conducts creative work involving everything from two- and three-dimensional works to video and space design. Daikoku was the recipient of the JAGDA New Designer Award, the Tokyo ADC Prize and the D&AD Yellow Pencil Awards.

P090

Daniel Renda

www.danielrenda.com

Daniel Renda is an independent art director and designer currently working in New York City. His current focuses are branding, identity, and applying design to lifestyle activities that he finds interesting. He has worked in the past designing for television and web advertising. He is classically trained as a graphic designer and enjoys various types of illustration.

P130

Deria Ormantzi

www.behance.net/deriaormantzi

Deria Ormantzi is a German designer experienced in graphic design.

P059

Designliga

www.designliga.com

Designliga is a bureau for visual communication and interior design. Working in a cross-disciplinary manner and communicating content through design, Designliga gets to the heart of brands and develops inspiring solutions that bring companies and products to life at their spatial, graphic and digital touchpoints. Their team of experienced designers, consultants and interior designers develops corporate identity and corporate design projects and creates spatial branding measures for interior architecture such as retail design and trade fair design.

P194-195

Deutsche & Japaner

http://deutscheundjapaner.com

With a distinct focus on holistic solutions, branding and corporate design as well as editorial and online performances, Deutsche & Japaner sets a high value on sustainable experiences. Passionate about detail, independent of any physical condition, the studio offers expertise in various disciplines, including interior design and scenography as well as conceptual creation, art direction and strategic brand escort.

P066-067

Dot Dash

www.thisisdotdash.com

Dot Dash is a new design and communications studio based in London, set up by Laura Walpole and Justin Hallström. Combining traditional design values with modern con¬ceptual thinking they strive to add real value to the businesses and organizations they work with. Approaching each project with a passion that takes both their clients and themselves, they are on a creative journey to deliver truly impactful visual solutions. Above all, they believe that great design comes from curious minds, collaboration and cre¬ativity. Dot Dash specializes in identity design, print, editorial, environmental, web, packaging and art direction.

P042-043

E

Empatia®

www.helloempatia.com

Back to purity, back to simplicity. Simplify to shine. Empatia® is an Argentinian-based design agency operating in a global marketplace. Together with the clients Empatia® makes brands live and profitable, and seeks the highest possible design quality down to the last detail. Long lasting and environmental, its design contributes towards economic and social sustainability.

P014-015, P020-021, P102-103

Enzed

www.enzed.ch

Enzed is a design consultancy based in Switzerland and run by Mélanie & Nicolas Zentner. It was founded in 2001 and specializes in the permanent quest for the remarkable.

P136-137

Esmutuo

www.esmutuo.com

Esmutuo is a Mediterranean design studio founded by Javier Alonso and based in Barcelona, Spain. Esmutuo produces a diverse range of work across multiple disciplines including print design, identity, app and web. Esmutuo creates content and mobilizing ideas, always with a clear and functional design. As communication has crossed the border of advertising and become a social fact, Esmutuo regards communication as something powerful and mighty.

P082-083

Esther Li

www.estherlidesign.com

Esther Li is a Senior studying Communications Design at Pratt Institute in Brooklyn, NY. She has participated in internships at Control Group, Mother NY, Sagmeister & Walsh and RoAndCo Studio. Apart from design she is also a figure skater and a diehard Patriots fan. She is available for freelance projects.

P100-101

Estudio FBDI

www.estudiofbdi.com

FBDI is a creative studio with its offices located in Buenos Aires, Argentina. Their goal is to provide every project and client with original ideas that express and represent the brand's potential. FBDI believes in the high impact of ideas and design and applies this concept to branding and brand communication. Federico Batemarco, the studio's director, founded FBDI over ten years ago with the intention of creating and enhancing national and international brands through graphic and industrial design and art direction. With incalculable experience in luxury and fashion brands, the studio works in different industries and segments.

P061, P200-201

F

Fabio Ongarato Design

www.fabioongaratodesign.com.au

Founded in 1992 by partners Fabio Ongarato and Ronnen Goren, based in Melbourne, Fabio Ongarato Design is renowned for the diversity of its work. The studio takes an open approach to graphic design, operating across a variety of graphic disciplines, from print to exhibitions to advertising. FOD's approach to design reflects their passion for architecture, photography and contemporary art. They work across a variety of fields such as fashion, corporate, arts and architecture deliberately crossing the boundaries between them.

P160-161, P186-187

Fabrice Le Nezet

www.fabricelenezet.com

Fabrice Le Nezet is a designer, visual artist and filmmaker based in London. His work explores the intersection between Architecture, Fashion and Toys Design through the use of raw material such as concrete and metal. The most recognizable in his work is the pure, clean and graphical aesthetic combined with playful qualities. In 2013, Fabrice Le Nezet founded the eponym creative studio to support his various researches in Graphic Design, Industrial Design and Sculpture.

P151

Firmalt

www.firmalt.com

Firmalt is a multidisciplinary design studio that provides unique creative solutions that develop and position brands. Firmalt creates strong visual concepts that communicate clear ideas, add value, and differentiate from the competition. Today, it has a portfolio with more than 50 projects in a variety of industries. Moreover, due to its great growth potential, it plans to expand its array of service offerings to provide even more complete and integral solutions for branding and communication.

P118

Foreign Policy Design Group

http://foreignpolicydesign.com

Foreign Policy Design Group is a team of idea makers & story tellers who help clients and brands realize and evolve their brands with creative and strategic deployment of traditional terrestrial channel & digital media channels. Helmed by Creative Directors Yah-Leng Yu and Arthur Chin, the group works on a good smorgasbord of projects ranging from creative/art direction and design, branding, brand strategy, digital strategy, strategic research and marketing campaign services for luxury fashion and lifestyle brands, fast-moving consumer goods brands, arts and cultural institution as well as think tank consultancies.

P088-089, P134-135

G

Glasfurd & Walker

www.glasfurdandwalker.com

Glasfurd & Walker is a design company that offers services in various disciplines, such as graphic design, art direction, brand creation and communication. The studio was founded in early 2007 and works with an international client base. Their goal is simple: Empower clients with relevant, innovative, high quality work that helps their business flourish.

P138-139

Graphical House

www.graphicalhouse.co.uk

Graphical House is a design consultancy located in Glasgow producing thoughtful and beautifully crafted work across all applications – digital, analogue and environmental.

P222-223

H

Helmo

www.helmo.fr

Helmo is a graphic design studio located in France ran by Thomas Couderc and Clement Vauchez. They work with primary bold colors in a playful manner – creating unique and stunning designs. Their understanding of form, color, typography and pattern enables them to keep producing exceptional visual feast for the audiences.

P156-157

Hey

http://heystudio.es

Hey is a multidisciplinary design studio based in Barcelona, Spain, specializing in brand management and editorial design, packaging and interactive design. They share the profound conviction that good design means combining content, functionality, graphical expression and strategy. As a result, their clients are offered personal service based on mutual understanding and trust.

P012-013, P158, P211, P220-221

I

IS Creative Studio

www.iscreativestudio.com

IS Creative Studio is an independent creative studio with global vision. With simplicity as the operating philosophy IS Creative Studio delivers services in brand identity and development, art direction, packaging, printed matter, interactive design, animation, art projects, exhibitions, fashion and product design. IS stands for Secret Ingredient. Believing in innovation, the power of great design and collaboration, IS Creative Studio works with other creative minds. IS Creative Studio was established in January 2010 by Richars Meza.

P192-193

J

Jono Garrett

http://jonogarrett.com

Jono Garrett is a freelance designer and illustrator originally from Johannesburg, South Africa. Garrett works on a large variety of projects, but particularly enjoys branding jobs for small clients where he can combine traditional corporate branding with illustration. By close collaboration, Garrett wants to achieve something that's intensely personal, functional and relevant to the client's business.

P054

L

La Tigre

http://latigre.net

La Tigre is an independent media studio in Milano, directed by two designers Luisa Milani and Walter Molteni. Since its opening in 2009, La Tigre takes on a wide variety of projects of different nature, such as web, printing, branding, editing and illustrating, always exploring original and alternative solutions. The graphic language is precise, direct, and driven by the use of basic elements like color, geometry and typography. Thanks to their union with creative and semantic research, La Tigre produces highly communicative visual systems with strong identities.

P092-093

Lotta Nieminen

www.lottanieminen.com

Lotta Nieminen is an illustrator, graphic designer and art director from Helsinki, Finland. She has studied graphic design and illustration at the University of Art and Design Helsinki and the Rhode Island School of Design, and has worked as a freelancer in both fields since 2006. After working for fashion magazine *Trendi*, Pentagram Design and RoAndCo Studio, Lotta now runs her own New York-based studio. As an illustrator, Lotta is represented by illustration agency Agent Pekka.

In 2010, Lotta received the Art Directors Club Young Guns award and was selected by *Print* magazine for its annual New Visual Artists review, highlighting 20 international rising designers under the age of 30. In 2014, she was nominated for *Forbes* magazine's annual 30 Under 30 list in the Art and Design category. Lotta has given talks around the US and Europe. Her client list includes companies such as Hermès, *New York Times*, Volkswagen, IBM, United Airlines, International Herald Tribune, *Monocle*, *Newsweek*, *Wired UK*, *New York Magazine*, and *Bloomberg Businessweek*.

P104-105

Lucía Izco

www.behance.com/luciaizco

Lucía Izco is a freelance graphic designer based in Buenos Aires, Argentina. Currently doing a degree in Graphic Design, Izco focuses on editorial design and communication.

P120-121

M

MABAA™

http://mabaa.es

Founded by Jose Alvarez Barranco and Iria Cid Mascareñas, MABAA™ is a creative agency that provides strategic solutions in the field of architecture, interior design, branding and project management applied especially to the retail sector. Providing an added value to the space and product, MABAA™ meets the emerging need of renovation, design and distinction that the current market demands.

P131, P166-167

Marcin Szmidt

http://marcinszmidt.com

Nominated and awarded in Project of the Year – Polish Design Award 2013, Marcin Szmidt is studying graphic design in Poland. Inspired by Bauhaus and De Stijl, Szmidt is fascinated with modernism, Swiss graphic design and concrete buildings.

P112

Maria Jose

www.behance.net/majomujermaravilla

Maria Jose was born and raised in a small town called Hermosillo in northern Mexico. Jose was already one of the founders of an agency when she was a student of a Monterrey-based university. But after two years and a half Jose decided to leave in order to learn to work elsewhere. Her curiosity makes it difficult for her to live in the same place. Currently Jose lives and works in Sydney.

P206-207, P224

Mariëlle van Genderen, Cathelijn Kruunenberg

http://mariellevangenderen.nl, www.cathelijnkruunenberg.nl

Mariëlle van Genderen and Cathelijn Kruunenberg are working as editorial designers for Frame Publishers, an internationally renowned publisher of the magazines *Frame*, *Mark* and *Elephant*, and many books on art, design and architecture. Within the company they are responsible for the art direction of *Frame* magazine, a bi-monthly publication about interior design, and *Mark* magazine, a bi-monthly publication about architecture. The main interest focuses on the constitutive relationship between typography, color and material in editorial design. Beside Frame Publishers they are working as an autonomous designer on self-initiated and commissioned design projects.

P074-075

Marina Soto

www.marinasoto.com

Born in 1990, Marina Soto is a graphic designer from Barcelona. Soto graduated at Escola Superior de Disseny (Universitat Ramon Llull, Barcelona) in 2013 and always likes to make books, posters, corporate identity, and websites. Combining her work with other freelance projects, Soto is currently working at graphic design studio Artofmany.

P128-129

Marius Wathne

www.mariuswathne.com

Marius Wathne is a Norwegian graphic designer with a degree in Communication Design from RMIT University, Melbourne.

P181

Marta Vargas

www.martavargas.com

Currently living in Stockholm, Sweden, graphic designer Marta Vargas was born in Barcelona, Spain. Vargas graduated in Graphic Design from Elisava Design School in 2012, and also studied at HDK School of Design and Crafts in Gothenburg, Sweden, as an exchange student in 2010. Vargas is working as a designer for Lupo Design (Stockholm), but previously she worked at the graphic design department of Elisava Design School and also served as an art director of the magazine of the same school.

P052

Masquespacio

http://masquespacio.com

Masquespacio is a creative consultancy that designs new experiences for brands and their customers through intelligent and creative tools for communication. The design firm led, by Ana Milena Hernández Palacios, has been recognized internationally for their innovative and unique interior design and branding projects.

P032-033, P094, P208-210, P212-215

Maximiliano Passarelli

www.behance.net/maxipassarelli

Maximiliano Passarelli is a young student of Graphic Design at the University of Buenos Aires, FADU. Investigating in his early career, Passarelli discovered his love towards typography. Pure and simple, his designs are based on geometric shapes and bright colors. Considering simplicity as an efficient way of communication, Passarelli loves white.

P022-023

MenosUnoCeroUno

http://menosunocerouno.com

MenosUnoCeroUno is an advertising agency, a branding boutique, and a digital agency integrated as a "one-stop-shop."

P034-035

Mildred & Duck

http://mildredandduck.com

Mildred & Duck is a small Melbourne-based graphic design studio, run by Sigiriya Brown and Daniel Smith. Established in 2011, Mildred & Duck works across a mix of industry sectors and design disciplines, with a range of different clients with varied budgets and requirements. Mildred & Duck works closely with their clients to ensure great results that exceed everyone's expectations.

P096-097

Mind Design
www.minddesign.co.uk

Mind Design is an independent graphic design studio based in East London. The studio was established in 1999 and specializes in the development of visual identities which includes print, web, packaging, signage and interior graphics. Mind Design is run by Holger Jacobs and Stewart Walker. Their approach combines hand-on craftmanship, conceptual thinking and most importantly, intuition. Visual ideas are often developed on the basis of research into production processes or the use of unusual materials.

P080, P178-179

moodley brand identity
www.moodley.at

moodley brand identity is an owner-led, award-winning strategic design agency with offices in Vienna and Graz. Since 1999 moodley has worked together with their customers to develop corporate and product brands which live, breathe and grow. moodley believes that their key contribution is to analyze complex requirements and develop simple, smart solutions with emotional appeal – whether corporate start-up, product launch or brand positioning. The team currently consists of about 60 employees from 7 different countries.

P053, P062-063, P081,

O

Ostecx Créative
http://ostecx.com

Ostecx Créative specializes in communication, without separating the activities that create a dialogue between a brand and consumers. Their portfolio includes traditional advertising campaigns, elements of visual identification, on-line promotions, and unconventional campaigns like experiential marketing. Ostecx Créative understands the role of an agency that aims to offer a complete range of advertising services, as successfully expressing the spirit of a brand in all the available communication channels, and exploring new ways of reaching consumers.

P018-019

P

p576
http://www.p576.com

p576 is a design studio based in Bogota, Colombia. They believe that through aesthetics they can help make a more beautiful and honest world.

P050-051

P·A·R
www.p-a-r.net

P·A·R is a graphic design studio located in Barcelona, grounded by Iris Tarraga and Lucía Castro in 2011. Starting from the concept of generating graphic communication elements, P·A·R offers solutions adapted to their customers' needs. Regarding communication and team work as their methodologies, P·A·R takes care of balance and harmony to create a functional design that fits with all disciplines.

P124-125

PalauGea
www.palaugea.com

PalauGea is a communication agency based in Spain. Palaugea has a multidisciplinary team of professionals who work together to realize communication projects. PalauGea takes care even of the smallest detail. PalauGea provides simple, yet durable responses in time.

P119

Patrick Fry
www.patrickfry.co.uk

Patrick Fry is an independent designer and art director from London. His practice works with a broad range of clients and disciplines, including everything from editorial and branding to interiors and animation. The studio is characterized by idea led visuals that are individually crafted for his clients and do not conform to a house style. The work is driven by a belief in collaboration, strong communication and unique outcomes. Recent clients include Paul Smith, Nike, BBC, Shakespeare's Globe, and Royal Albert Hall plus a variety of smaller start ups and socially responsible organizations.

P132-133

Paulo Lopes
www.paulolopes.org

Independent design studio Paulo Lopes Studio is able to reach where others can't fit. Paulo Lopes Studio specializes in unique and innovative graphics, contemporary and content-driven visual communication, working with cultural institutions, open-minded individuals and committed corporations.

P185

Planet Creative
www.planetcreative.com

Planet Creative was founded in 2004 and is located in Stockholm, Sweden. Planet Creative is a branding agency focusing on corporate culture and visual identities. From idea to execution, their work covers the entire brand building chain.

P144-145

Q

Querida Studio
www.querida.si

Querida Studio is a design and communication studio based in Barcelona. In Spain, people use the word "querida" to refer to the lover, the woman that they love and want, the one that strikes their passion. And that's how Querida Studio likes to see the projects they work on: little or great love stories with brands and institutions. Querida Studio loves typography, illustration, colors, photography and enjoys new technologies as much as they worship detail and craft.

P106-107

Quim Marin
http://quimmarin.com

Quim Marin is a designer based in Barcelona, Spain. Marin's work is strongly linked to the show business, music in particular.

P216-217

R

Raw Color
www.rawcolor.nl

Raw Color is a collaboration of two designers Christoph Brach and Daniera ter Haar. Their work reflects a sophisticated treatment of material through the mixing of the fields of photography and graphic design. This aesthetic is reflected through the research and experiments used to build their visual language. In their Eindhoven based studio they are working on self-initiated and commissioned projects. Driven by curiosity they are questioning the meaning of the subject they are working on. Within these aspects the materialization of color plays a key role, and can be seen as the core of the studio.

P031, P140-141, P176-177, P230-232

Ray Yen
www.behance.net/rayyen

Ray Yen was born in Taipei, Taiwan. He majored in Commercial Design at Chung Yuan Christian University. He is a freelance graphic designer specialized in brand, corporate identity design, typography design and Packaging design.

P038-039

RE
www.re-blog.co

RE is a collective of ambitious idealists, trying to change the world through branding. RE works with ambitious clients to build notorious brands.

P110-111, P148-149

RoAndCo
http://roandcostudio.com

RoAndCo, founded in 2006 and led by award-winning Creative Director Roanne Adams, is a multi-disciplinary creative agency that serves as a visual thought leader for a range of forward-thinking fashion and lifestyle clients. As branding experts, Roanne and her team work quickly and intuitively to pinpoint the most essential, visceral quality with which to tell a company's story and visually captivate its audience. As creative – whose services include graphic design and art direction for print, web, and video – they're known for bringing clients a cool cachet and a contemporary look while remaining grounded in a love of the classics, from old movie typography to modernist art to the work of mid-century design icons. With a diverse roster of talents hailing from Brazil to Japan, the agency aims to thoughtfully distill a client's inspirations, ideas and motivations into fresh, sincere and compelling brand messages that engage and resonate.

P024-025

S

Salma Shamel
www.behance.net/salmashamel

Salma Shamel is Cairo-based designer experienced in graphic

design. Shamel's work ranges from naming and art direction to graphic design and creation of advertising campaigns.

P202-203

Sam Curtis

www.samcurtis.co.uk

Sam Curtis often adapts his practice and skills depending on the individual brief. Within these briefs Curtis tends to experiment with neat, clean and ordered imagery, often informed by his passion for design and typography. His background in photography has heavily informed his current practice; Curtis often incorporates old photographs that carry either personal or project-relevant connotations. More recently, his interests (and client work) have expanded into brand identity, advertising, packaging and art direction, with a strong graphic focus on digital rendering.

P072-073

Sherman Chia J.W

www.shermanjw.com

Unlike most graphic designers, Sherman Chia J.W began his life as a Marketing person. Sherman has always loved design but soon after completing his diploma, Sherman decided to pursue his dream of design communication in university. Sherman has always loved challenging the brief and redefining the traditional. His focus lies mainly in packaging and branding. "My work methodology is that I prefer an open mind when approaching each brief and explore as wildly as possible. Then I will rope myself back in and go through my ideas. As a creative, I stand that 'if you don't go all out to discover the moon, how do you know that it's possible.' I draw my inspiration from everything and anything such as architecture, typography, music, food blogs and even just window shopping," said Sherman.

P055, P058

Simon Laliberte

www.atelierbangbang.ca

Simon Laliberte is a screen-printer and graphic designer from Montreal, Quebec. Laliberte graduated in Graphic Design from the University of Quebec at Montreal. Laliberte is specialized in branding & identity, packaging, print design and screen-printing.

P098-099

SmartHeart

http://smart-heart.ru

SmartHeart is an independent agency that creates integrated projects in the field of branding, design and advertising. SmartHeart creates a product based on rational and emotional approaches: the harmonious combination of logic (smart) and emotions (heart).

P168-169

smbetsmb

www.smbetsmb.com

Keita Shimbo and Misaco Shimbo are running a design studio named "smbetsmb" in Tokyo, Japan. They design for companies, exhibitions and trade fairs. Their work includes information systems, books and posters.

P086-087

Stephanie Helou

www.behance.net/helou

Stephanie Helou believes in complexity and discipline. Helou cares more about the process rather than results, understanding a problem rather than coming up with a preset solution. Helou thinks that being a designer is being part of the world and it keeps oneself sensitive to changes, movement and flows.

P226-227

Studio8585

www.studio8585.com

Studio8585 is a Croatian design studio which develops bespoke visual identities, responsive websites and other associated materials including stationery, books, posters, brochures and signage for international and local clients. Agile and effective, small but ambitious, Studio8585 is driven by rationality and devoted to delivering crafted, elegant & functional visual experiences with expressive bite.

P172-173

T

The Folks Studio

www.thefolksstudio.com

The Folks Studio is a design practice based in Singapore and was founded by Yang & Siew in 2012. Derived from the Germanic noun fulka, folks means people, and serves as a constant reminder that people are at the core of their thinking and in what they do.

P078

Trapped in Suburbia

www.trappedinsuburbia.com

"Tell me and I'll forget; show me and I may remember, involve me and I'll understand." Focusing on human interaction and engaging your audience, design studio Trapped in Suburbia takes their clients on a graphic journey and surprises them.

P190-191

Two Times Elliott

http://2xelliott.co.uk

Two Times Elliott is a design consultancy based in Notting Hill, London. Two Times Elliott produces a diverse range of work across multiple disciplines, including print design, identity and web. They help their clients communicate their message clearly and intelligently.

P046

V

Veronica Vespertine S.

http://classes.dma.ucla.edu/Spring14/161/projects/veronica/7-portfolio/html

Veronica Vespertine S. is a graphic designer based on Los Angeles and Beijing. She graduated from Beijing No.4 High School and is currently majoring in Design and Media Arts and Architecture at UCLA. Her works usually involves in multi-media, including print, graphic motion, web design, interactive design, game design and photography. The majority of them investigate the relation between content, information, and color. She has been recognized by various design institutions including Behance, Adobe Design Awareness Award, Cargo, etc., and her works have been exhibited multiple times at the New Wright Gallery at Los Angeles.

P056-057

Very Own Studio

http://veryownstudio.com

Very Own Studio is an independent creative practice established by Mark Ferguson in 2009, based in Brighton on the south coast of England. It helps clients turn ambitions, aspirations and values into the visible face of their business, working with them to discover, create and communicate a visual story that thrives within today's fast moving environment. At Very Own Studio the belief is that good design can inspire, influence thinking and even change the way people live. The studio has a reputation for creating confident, timeless and

thoughtful design that is effective and compelling, exuding elegance and simplicity.

P009-011

W

Werklig

www.werklig.com

Werklig is an independent brand design agency founded in 2008. Their office is located in Helsinki, but they serve more than 50 clients both in Finland and internationally. They are designers, creatives and consultants – but most of all, they are problem solvers.

P198

Z

Zaky Arifin

http://zakyarifin.com/

Born in 1983, Zaky Arifin is a Jakarta-based graphic designer and visual artist. His work ranges from brand identity, typeface, typography experiment to custom lettering, chalk mural and visual art. His work is a journey of simplicity.

P204-205

Acknowledgements

We would like to express our gratitude to all of the designers and companies for their generous contribution of images, ideas, and concepts. We are also very grateful to many other people whose names do not appear in the credits but who made specific contributions and provided support. Without them, the successful completion of this book would not be possible. Special thanks to all of the contributors for sharing their innovation and creativity with all of our readers around the world. Our editorial team includes editor Zhaohong Yang and book designer Dongyan Wu, to whom we are truly grateful.